阿 拉 善 SEE 基 金 会 资 助 出 版

多样性的中国荒漠 DIVERSE DESERTS OF CHINA

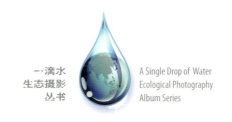

一滴水生态摄影丛书

A Single Drop of Water Ecological Photography Album Series

多样性的中国荒漠
DIVERSE DESERTS OF CHINA

陈建伟 著／摄

CHEN JIANWEI

中国林业出版社

CHINA FORESTRY PUBLISHING HOUSE

图书在版编目（CIP）数据

多样性的中国荒漠 / 陈建伟著、摄. -- 北京：中国林业出版社，2017.8
ISBN 978-7-5038-9207-3

Ⅰ. ①多… Ⅱ. ①陈… Ⅲ. ①摄影集－中国－现代②荒漠－中国－摄影集 Ⅳ. ① J421

中国版本图书馆 CIP 数据核字（2017）第 171042 号

责任编辑：肖静
特约编辑：田红
英文翻译：柴晚锁　李超　李佳芯　李鹏云　宋军　王静
英文审校：郭瑜富
图片编辑：黄晓凤　王静
装帧设计：黄华强
制　　作：北京睿宸弘文文化传播有限公司
审 图 号：GS(2017)2189 号

出版：中国林业出版社（100009 北京西城区刘海胡同 7 号）
E-mail：wildlife_cfph@163.com
电话：（010）83225764
印刷：北京雅昌艺术印刷有限公司
版次：2017 年 8 月第 1 版
印次：2017 年 8 月第 1 次
开本：787mm×1092mm　1/12
印张：18
定价：280.00 元

荒漠大写意之一　"旷野苍茫"·甘肃祁连山麓
干旱环境里，在千万年风蚀、水蚀的反复作用下，地球表面镌刻了荒漠的万道褶皱、千古沧桑。

Desert Landscape One "Vast Wilderness" — Foothills of Qilian Mountain, Gansu
In the arid environment, repeated erosion of wind and water over millennia has left the surface of the Earth engraved with uncountable folds and furls of rolling deserts, telling of the vicissitudes and changes that this planet has undergone.

荒漠大写意之二 "沙水之间"·内蒙古巴丹吉林沙漠

在这里，沙丘与湖面相映相伴，沙丘越是高大，湖面越是宽广。沙、水、人一起印证着大自然的对立统一规律，共同演奏着华丽的生态乐章。

Desert Landscape Two "Where the Sands Meet the Water" — Badan Jaran Desert, Inner Mongolia

Here, dunes and the lakes form sharp contrasts. The taller the dunes are, the wider the lakes are. The sands, the water and human beings live in perfect harmony, testifying to the fundamental law of nature — uniformity disguised in contrasts — and celebrating the magnificent scores of the natural ecological system.

荒漠大写意之三 "戈壁精灵"·宁夏贺兰山
戈壁岩石虽然苍凉，但各种生物活跃依然。突然，一群岩羊在你的面前跳跃而过，你不得不感叹荒漠生命竟如此顽强。

Desert Landscape Three "The Elves of Gobi" —Helan Mountains, Ningxia
Regardless of the desolate and barren landscape, lives thrive among the rocks in the Gobi. As a flock of bharals pop unexpectedly up into and then soon vanish from one's sight, one surely cannot but marvel at the tenacity and vitality of lives in the deserts.

荒漠大写意之四 "远古洪荒"·内蒙古古居延海
当你走到这里，好像看见了万年大自然莫测的变幻。这里曾经是湖泊？曾经是高山？你有幸在这里和它相遇，你就融入了历史，融入了亘古的自然。

Desert Landscape Four "Time Immemorial" — Ancient Juyan Lake, Inner Mongolia
As you get closer, you would feel as if the mysterious history over millennia were unfolding right in front of you. What a scene it used to be in time immemorial, vast lakes or insurmountable mountains? Is it predestined that you will inevitably come across it here, and hence make yourself an integral part of the endless history of the eternal nature?

荒漠大写意之五"生命吉祥"·新疆库姆塔格沙漠
人们也许很难理解,这里就是野骆驼的天堂。这只奔跑的野骆驼正在换毛,展示了自然的季节变换。大漠荒荒,干热缺水凄凉,而它们就是这里的主人,人类现代文明在这里的表现就是不打扰它们。愿荒漠里的生命永远安康吉祥!

Desert Landscape Five "Auspicious Life" — Kumtag Desert, Xinjiang
It might appear incredible that this could be a haven where wild camels thrive. The wild camel in the picture, following the call of seasonal alternation in the nature, is undergoing molting. In the dry, hot and desolate desert landscape, wild camels have over thousands of years adapted themselves to the environment and made the deserts their promised home. The best that we, the civilized modern human beings, can do under this awe-inspiring setting is to restrain ourselves from intruding into their habitats, and to wish in silence. May they thrive and prosper forever in the deserts!

序一

森林、湿地、荒漠生态系统是地球陆地最重要的三大自然生态系统。它们都是大自然中历经千万年形成的、不可或缺的重要组成部分。荒漠生态系统有如防风固沙、土壤保育、水资源调控、生物多样性保护、初级土壤提供、沙尘全球环境增益等生态功能。相比较其他生态系统，荒漠生态系统更显脆弱，一旦受气候原因和人们的干扰破坏，退化容易恢复难。荒漠生态系统是中国最重要的陆地生态系统之一，它的生态服务功能在我国干旱、半干旱的西北地区尤显重要。

没有对荒漠生态系统的正确认识，就不可能在防治荒漠化方面有正确的思想指导和有效措施。而荒漠化就是荒漠生态系统服务功能的退化或者丧失，森林、湿地、草地生态系统崩溃或严重退化在一定条件下也会形成荒漠化，荒漠化被称为"地球的癌症"，治理荒漠化就是恢复由于荒漠化而丧失的生态系统服务功能。中国政府历来高度重视荒漠化的防治工作，并积极履行《联合国防治荒漠化公约》的义务。特别是党的十八大做出"大力推进生态文明建设"的重大战略决策以来，我国防治荒漠化的工作在加强制度建设、政策支持、工程治理等方面都取得了积极进展，先后编制实施了《全国防沙治沙规划》，出台了沙化土地封禁保护制度，继续实施了京津风沙源治理、三北防护林体系、退耕还林、天然林资源保护、野生动植物保护和自然保护区建设等重大工程，开展了自然保护区、沙化土地封禁区和国家沙漠公园的建设，进一步强化了防沙治沙执法检查和省级政府防沙治沙任期目标责任考核工作，成功举办了世界防治荒漠化与干旱日全球纪念活动暨"一带一路"高级别对话。通过一系列强有力的举措，在荒漠化防治领域，尊重自然、保护自然、师法自然的生态文明理念逐步增强，政府企业公众共治的行动体系逐步形成，我国荒漠化防治步伐不断加快，并取得了明显的成效。自2000年以来，全国荒漠化和沙化土地面积连续三个监测期保持"双减少"，荒漠化土地面积由20世纪末年均扩展1.04万km^2转变为目前的年均缩减2424 km^2，沙化土地面积由20世纪末年均扩展3436 km^2转变为目前的年均缩减1980 km^2，实现了由"沙进人退"到"人进沙退"的历史性转变，为推进生态文明和美丽中国建设做出了积极的贡献。同时，也为国际社会治理荒漠生态环境树立了标杆，贡献了"中国智慧"和"中国经验"。

习近平总书记提出，"要坚持保护优先、自然恢复为主，开展大规模国土绿化行动，加快水土流失和荒漠化石漠化综合治理"，并提出要践行绿色发展的新理念，就推动形成绿色发展方式和生活方式提出重点任务，牢固树立"绿水青山就是金山银山"的强烈意识。国家林业局承担了我国生态保护和建设主战场的重任，森林、湿地、荒漠生态系统及野生动植物保护即"三大系统一个多样性"是国家林业局党组对于全局工作的基本定位。我们要举全局之力，上下一心，为实现人民富裕、国家富强、祖国美丽的中国梦而努力。

陈建伟同志几十年来一直从事生态系统及生物多样性保护的调查监测、科研及管理工作，曾担任过中国荒漠化监测中心首任常务副主任，组织过全国第一次荒漠化调查，之后又长期从事自然保护工作。工作需要摄影，摄影促进工作，他结合自身的工作经历和知识，坚持用生态文明的理念来思考和解读中国的自然保护工作，运用生态摄影的创新思维，先后出版了《多样性的中国森林》《多样性的中国湿地》生态摄影集。为迎接今年《联合国防治荒漠化公约》第十三次缔约方大会在中国的召开，又将出版《多样性的中国荒漠》生态摄影集。这本书在充分论证的基础上，从生态系统的角度，对中国荒漠区划及区域特点做了有益的探索和展示，并提出了对于荒漠生态系统保护及防治荒漠化工作的生态思考。本书图片丰富精美、文字洗练，既能给读者带来对荒漠生态系统广博、粗犷、大美的感受，又有益于提高大众对荒漠生态系统重要性的认识，并引起社会对于防治荒漠化的更多关注。本书的正式出版实现了作者本人做齐中国森林、湿地、荒漠三大系统生态摄影集的夙愿，值得祝贺。

希望我们每一个人都积极行动起来，尽己所能为中国荒漠生态系统的保护和防治荒漠化建设贡献出自己的一份力量，为建设美丽中国而努力奋斗。

国家林业局局长
2017年7月

Forward I

Forests, wetlands and deserts are the three most critical natural terrestrial ecological systems on the Earth that have been shaped by the nature over billions of years. Desert ecosystems provide us with multiple ecological services, like sand fixation, soil conservation, water resources regulation, biodiversity conservation, rudimentary soil making, as well as global environment enrichment with sand dust. However, compared with other ecological systems, desert ecosystems are more vulnerable, and it would be very hard for them to recover once being destroyed. Extensively acknowledged as one of the most critical terrestrial ecosystems, desert ecosystems and the eco-services they provide are of particular significance to the arid and semi-arid regions in North-western China.

Without a sound scientific recognition of the desert ecosystem, it would be hardly possible for us to come up with either proper approaches or effective methods in combating desertification. Desertification, which refers to the deterioration or total loss of eco-services provided by deserts and hence is sometimes compared to "cancer of the Earth", might also be caused by continuous, serious deterioration of overused forest, wetland or grassland ecosystems. The prevention of desertification means to contain the spread of human-inflicted deterioration and loss of desert eco-services, and in turn to recover those that have deteriorated or lost. The Chinese government has consistently attached great importance to combating desertification and to honoring its commitments to the United Nations Convention to Combat Desertification. The 18th CPC National Congress identified "promoting the development of ecological civilization" as one of China's key strategic policy, which has ushered the country in a new historic period during which major progresses were made in both policy-making and program implementations.

In addition to the consecutive promulgation of the *National Plan for Desertification Prevention and Control*, and an entire set of rules/regulations concerning the protection of sandy lands, a wide range of programs were implemented, including the "Sandstorm Source Control in Areas in Vicinity of Beijing and Tianjin", the "Three North Shelterbelt Development Program", the "Land Conversion Program", the "Natural Forest Protection Program", the "Wildlife Conservation Program", and the "Nature Reserve Development Program" to name just a few. The development of nature reserves, sandy land enclosure zone and national desert parks has been enhanced. Inspections of law-enforcement in combating desertification and assessments of the set goals of each provincial government in desertification combating and prevention have been further strengthened. World Combating Desertification Day—the Belt and Road Initiative High Level Dialogue has also been held with a great success. Thanks to the above-mentioned efforts and initiatives, people's ecological civilization awareness—which features "respecting the nature, conserving nature and following the natural laws"— has been greatly enhanced, and mechanisms conducive to tri-party (government-business-individual) cooperation have been put in place to quicken up the country's paces for combating desertification. Over the three consecutive monitoring terms since 2000, a "double declining trend" in the sizes of both desertified and sandified lands in China has been steadily maintained, with the average annual expanding rates cut respectively down to -2424 km^2 and -1980 km^2, as against 10400 km^2 and 3436 km^2 at the end of the last century. The historic transition from a "desert-prevailing" trend to a "human-prevailing" trend testifies not just to the major achievements that China has made in its drive to boost eco-civilization, but also to the remarkable contributions it has made to the international community in upgrading the desert ecosystems through the application of "Chinese wisdom" and "Chinese expertise".

President Xi Jinping urged us to "give priority to conservation-oriented efforts and to resort primarily to the self-recovery capacity of nature in our campaign to conduct large scale land greening and accelerate the comprehensive control over water and soil erosion, land desertification and land degradation in rocky areas". He also called on us to, through putting into practice new ideas about green growth, set clear objectives in promoting green modes of development and living, and firmly build the strong awareness of "treasuring the clear water and green hills as mountains of gold and silver". The State Forestry Administration, the taskforce of China's ecological conservation and progress endeavor, has identified as its ultimate goal to put the country's forest, wetland and desert ecosystems and biodiversity under effective protection. We pledge our whole-hearted commitment in bringing into reality our much-aspired China dream—a well-off population, a thriving nation, and a beautiful homeland.

Mr. Chen Jianwei has over the past few decades been actively engaged in monitoring, researching and managing the ecological systems and biodiversity of our country. During his term as the founding Executive Deputy Director General of China Desertification Monitoring Center, he organized the first national desert inventory, which marked just the beginning of his life long career in nature conservation. Drawing on his extensive exposure to state-of-the-art ideas concerning eco-civilization and abundant personal experiences nature conservation, he has previously published two ecological albums, *Diverse Forests of China* and *Diverse Wetlands of China*. The present one among his series, *Diverse Deserts of China*, which shall be dedicated as his tribute to the upcoming COP 13 of the United Nations Convention to Combat Desertification, marks another noteworthy achievement he has made in this field. In addition to the breathtaking pictures, his thorough studies on deserts across the country, his insightful reflections on our previous and future work in combating desertification and desert ecosystem protection, all makes this an especially valuable and worthwhile book. Besides presenting to us such impressive, awesome vistas of the deserts, it also serves as an enlightening book for us to get better understanding about the critical roles they play in protecting the integrity and health of the overall global ecosystem, hence enhancing people's awareness in this regard. For Mr. Chen himself, the publication of this book is of particular significance, since it marked the fulfillment of his long term aspiration—completing his eco-album series about the three major terrestrial ecosystems, i.e. that of forests, wetlands and deserts. I would like to extend my most heartfelt congratulations to him for this great accomplishment.

It is sincerely hope that each of us readers shall draw inspiration from his worthy book and do his share in our shared endeavor for desert ecosystem protection and desertification combating in a bid to build a beautiful China.

ZHANG JIANLONG
Administrator, State Forestry Administration, P. R. C
July 2017

序二

反映中国荒漠生态系统的书不少，但是象《多样性的中国荒漠》这种形式反映中国荒漠生态系统的书却不多。该书用丰富多彩的图片，加上洗练简明的文字，给大家进行了一次多样性中国荒漠的科普活动。这种用生态摄影的新理念来给读者讲述一个生动的中国荒漠故事的方法值得赞赏。尤其是该书不仅仅是尽力满足了视觉上的艺术呈现、知识上的科学道理，更重要的是提出了问题，促进了人们思想上的生态思考。

我很早就认识陈建伟先生，他开始是从事技术业务工作的，对于当时林业系统开展森林、湿地、荒漠、野生动植物调查监测做了很多开创性的工作，后来调到现国家林业局机关从事自然保护的行政管理，技术业务工作打下的基础也帮助他在行政管理方面有所建树。他能够以一己之力陆续将中国森林、中国湿地、中国荒漠生态系统的多样性以生态摄影的方式编辑出版，显示了他几十年在自然生态方面学习钻研和积累的功夫，并不简单。书中既有对于前人科研工作的继承应用，又有自己的创新和思考；既有生动画面的观赏性又具文字表述的知识性、科学性。就如他开创并提倡的生态摄影一样，蕴藏的是思想性、科学性、艺术性统一的新理念，讲述的是多样性的中国生态故事。

我认为这本书在讲述多样性的中国荒漠中有几点给人印象深刻。

一是始终强调用生态系统的观点来看待荒漠，认为没有对荒漠生态系统的正确认识，就不可能在防治荒漠化方面有正确的思想指导和有效的措施。并且强调，荒漠化就是荒漠生态系统服务功能的退化或者丧失，森林、湿地、草地生态系统崩溃或严重退化，在一定条件下也会形成荒漠化，而防治荒漠化就是要恢复由于人为原因而丧失和退化的生态系统服务功能。这个思想始终贯穿整本书的图片采用和文字论述之中。

二是在前人工作的基础上，大胆提出荒漠生态系统有如防风固沙、土壤保育、水资源调控、生物多样性保护、初级土壤提供、沙尘全球环境增益等生态服务功能，这个提法也是较新颖的。将荒漠比喻成地球的"脾"，用中华文化的五行来解释，脾主土，脾为气血生化之源、后天之本，主运化、造血，主要承担了自然界初级土壤制造和生物多样性保育等功能，这个提法尚待进一步探索。我们将森林比喻做"地球的肺"，把湿地比喻做"地球的肾",把荒漠比喻做"地球的脾",按照中华五行学说,肺主气,肾主水,脾主土,这样自然界气、液、固三状态,气、水、土三要素都全了。把地球比喻得像人一样的生命体,会让人感到更便于理解、更容易亲近,从而更愿意去珍惜它、爱护它,这是比喻的初衷。

三是在前人研究的基础上,经过大量实地调研,大胆将喜马拉雅山脉北麓、阿里地区等高寒干旱极干旱区划入荒漠的自然地理区域内,将原来荒漠区的南缘大大往南推进,并且讲述了提出它的道理,这个也算是从实际出发,不拘泥于框框的大胆尝试。

四是对于荒漠及荒漠化之间的关系做了认真的讲述,有助于大家理解"师法自然"的深刻内涵。不能再盲目地提出向沙漠进军,人定胜天等不符合科学的口号,但是也不是在自然面前无所作为、束手无策。提出"师法自然"的意思,就是我们只要遵循荒漠生态系统的内在规律去做,去下大力气,就可以取得防治荒漠化的巨大成果。自 2000 年以来,全国荒漠化和沙化土地面积连续三个监测期保持"双减少",实现了由"沙进人退"到"人进沙退"的历史性转变,中国这些年防治荒漠化取得的成果,就是遵照自然规律、师法自然的结果。

书中的一些观点和看法未必都是正确的,肯定也存在不少考虑不周全的地方,但是,用生态摄影的方法来讲述科学的道理和故事,这种方法值得鼓励,尤其是我们处于一个快节奏的读图时代,让公众在欣赏美丽图片的同时,了解到荒漠生态系统的科学知识,促进对于防治荒漠化的思考和积极的行动,这对于提高公众的生态环境保护意识大有裨益,对于传播生态文化、建设生态文明社会都是非常有利的。

中国科学院院士
2017年7月

Forward II

Books about the desert ecosystems in China abound, but those tell about such ecosystems in such an impressive and innovative means like *Diverse Deserts of China* are indeed rare. The extensive employment of breathtaking or thought-provoking photos, with the supplement of brief verbal explanations, in disseminating knowledge concerning the rich diversity of deserts found in China in vivid and memorable ways is really commendable. More importantly, this book is not valuable just for its aesthetical merits, or its solid basis in science, but for the serious ecological reflections it arouses in the hearts of the readers.

I have been a long-time friend of Mr. Chen Jianwei, who started his career as a forestry professional specialized in inventory and monitoring of the forest, wetland, desert and wildlife resources in China. The pioneering work and rich technical expertise gained in his early career turn out to be especially valuable when he was later on transferred to work on administrative posts in the State Forestry Administration (SFA), as showcased by the many major accomplishments he has made over the years. His unremitting efforts have resulted in the consecutive publication of a series of eco-albums that respectively feature on the rich diversity of forests, wetlands and deserts throughout China. The books are tributes to the major findings of previous studies, but also crystallizations of his own innovative reflections; they are artistic books excelling in aesthetical values, but also science books that disseminate knowledge in enlightening ways. He blazed a new way for telling about Chinese ecological stories through his camera, highlighting simultaneously their scientific, artistic as well as instructional functions.

Diverse Deserts of China is especially impressive to me in the following aspects.

First is its consistent stress on the needs to take deserts as integrated ecological systems. The author reiterates that without a sound scientific recognition of the desert ecosystem, it would be hardly possible for us to come up with either proper approaches or effective methods in combating desertification. He further emphasizes that desertification refers to the deterioration or total loss of eco-services provided by deserts. The collapse or serious degradation of forest, wetlands and grassland ecosystems would result in desertification under certain circumstances. The prevention of desertification, therefore, means to contain the spread of human-inflicted deterioration and loss of desert eco-services, and in turn to recover those that have deteriorated or lost. This viewpoint and train of thoughts runs throughout the entire book, both in the visual pictures and verbal descriptions.

Secondly, in addition to acknowledging findings from previous studies, the author also proposes an original perspective for evaluating deserts, highlighting their multiple ecological services, like sand fixation, soil conservation, water resources regulation, biodiversity conservation, rudimentary soil making, as well as global environment enhancement by sand dust. Borrowing from traditional Chinese wisdom concerning the functioning of human bodies, the author argues that: if the forest ecosystems are to be compared to the lungs of the Earth whose primary function are to provide us with fresh air and oxygen, and the wetland ecosystems to its kidneys responsible for cleaning and purifying waters, it would make sense for us to compare the desert ecosystems to its spleens, which are the starting points of air and blood circulations within human bodies and, similarly, responsible for decomposition, filtering and providing primary forms of soil in the natural systems of the planet. The application of this metaphor, which compares the Earth to human body, not only makes highly technical explanations about the functioning of the Earth much more accessible and vivid, but also appeals powerfully to readers' empathy for valuing, cherishing these systems.

Thirdly, drawing on previous studies and personal field observation, the author raises a bold proposal that expanded the desert zones of China further southward to include certain regions on the Qinghai-Tibet Plateau, such as the extremely cold and arid or super-arid parts at the north slope of the Himalayas, Ali, and *etc*. Reasons for such proposal are also clearly stated, making such bold vision worth particular attentions.

Fourthly, the dynamic relationship between deserts and desertification is seriously explored to drive home to its readers the significance of "respecting the inherent laws of nature". The abandonment of such foolhardy fantasies as "human-prevailing-over-nature" does not mean that we shall be reduced totally helpless and hopeless when confronted with adversary natural situations. By the principle of "respecting the inherent laws of nature", we mean that, so long as we following the natural laws of the desert ecosystems, notable achievements can be reached in our efforts for combating desertification. Over the three consecutive monitoring terms since 2000, a "double declining trend" has been steadily maintained in the sizes of both desertified and sandified lands in China. The historic transition from a "desert-prevailing" trend to a "human-prevailing" trend has been brought into reality. These are all the natural results of our consistent observance to the guiding principle of "respecting the inherent laws of nature".

For sure, not all the viewpoints and perspectives raised in the book are absolutely indisputable, and some of them still call for further verification through more rigorous scientific studies. But nevertheless, the creative approach for disseminating knowledge through eco-featuring photos is indeed a worthwhile attempt. In this fast-paced picture-reading era in which we are situated, this is especially the case. Besides the beautiful photos, readers are at the same time exposed to systematic knowledge concerning desert ecosystems, which in turn encourages them to reflect seriously on the meaning of combating desertification, hence enhancing their awareness for environmental protection. In short, the publication of this book shall be highly constructive to the promotion of eco-culture and development of eco-civilization.

LI WENHUA
Academician of Chinese Academy of Sciences
July 2017

前言

《多样性的中国荒漠》终于能和读者见面了，和前面出版的《多样性的中国森林》《多样性的中国湿地》相比，这本书出得更艰难一些，主要是因为荒漠生态系统方面可以借鉴的研究成果不多，仅是有关中国荒漠的自然地理区划就让我反复折腾一直到出正式书稿前，现地考察、查阅研究资料和请教专家是始终如一的必修课。我是中国荒漠化监测中心的创始人，组织过全国第一次荒漠化调查，后来又一直在从事森林、湿地、荒漠和野生动植物的调查监测、科研和管理工作，几十年出入祖国的大荒大漠甚至无人区并用相机记录下所经历的一切，再加上有了大家的热情支持和鼓励，这算是我敢于出这本生态摄影集的底气。

若把森林生态系统比喻为地球的"肺"，肺主气，主要承担了提供氧气、清新空气的功能；把湿地生态系统比喻为地球的"肾"，肾主水，主要承担了清洁、净化水的功能；那么我们也可以把荒漠生态系统比喻为地球的"脾"，脾主土，脾为气血生化之源，后天之本，主运化、造血，主要承担了自然界分解、过滤、提供初级土壤的功能。中国的荒漠并非极目荒凉的不毛之地，不仅有丰富的大漠、雅丹、戈壁、沙漠、荒漠草原、土林、沙湖、盐池、内流河、古城堡、古丝绸之路、沙漠绿洲等自然景观，而且有丰富的野生动物、植物和微生物资源。

而这些荒漠动植物种大多是在严酷的环境条件下经过长期自然选择而保留下来的，具有顽强的生命力和优良的遗传基因，其中还有一些是中国荒漠的特有种和珍稀种。这些野生动植物及其环境，构成了我国特殊的荒漠生态系统，在自然生态及生物多样性方面具有不可替代的重要价值。

由于人们对于荒漠的认识往往只停留在沙尘暴，沙埋庄稼与房舍，沙进人退等场景中，也因为荒漠干旱、荒芜、空旷且环境严酷，往往被人畏而远之视为生命禁区，并将荒漠化比喻为"地球的癌症"。因此，荒漠生态系统是一个人们最陌生、最畏惧、最不能正确认识的地球生态系统。对待荒漠和人之间的关系，人们往往没有一个正确的认识，一会要避而远之，一会要人定胜天，这些都是错误的。这些认识之所以错误，是没有把荒漠当作一个生态系统，一个自然界的客观存在来认识所产生的。荒漠生态系统有如防风固沙、土壤保育、水资源调控、生物多样性保护、初级土壤制造、沙尘全球环境增益等生态服务功能。为了保护这些荒漠珍贵资源、保护荒漠生态系统，目前中国已建立了一大批荒漠生态系统类型的自然保护区，其中有中外闻名的宁夏沙坡头自然保护区，有面积排在中国自然保护区前几名并有丰富荒漠野生动物资源的保护区，如西藏羌塘、珠峰，青海可可西里、青海湖，新疆卡拉麦里、阿尔金山、罗布泊，内蒙古额济纳，甘肃阿克塞、西湖等自然保护区。中国荒漠类型的自然保护区尽管在数量上比森林、湿地类型的自然保护区都少，但是其面积却是最大的，大约占到国土总面积的5%左右。

但是，荒漠生态系统是相当脆弱的，破坏容易恢复极难，在干旱、半干旱、半湿润地区，人们对于土地的过度利用就会引起土地的退化，即荒漠化。荒漠化就是荒漠生态系统服务功能的退化或者丧失，而防治荒漠化就是要保护和恢复荒漠生态系统的服务功能。没有一个对荒漠生态系统的正确认识，就不可能在防治荒漠化方面有正确的思想指导和有效的措施。对于这个问题，本书在每一章节里的都会谈到，在最后还专门设置了生态思考部分讲人与荒漠之间的关系。中国在防治荒漠化方面一直在不懈地努力，并取得了举世瞩目的成就，2017年"《联合国防治荒漠化公约》第十三次缔约方大会"在中国召开，是对中国在这方面取得成就的充分肯定。谨以本书献给此次大会，诚然，我个人的认识是粗浅的，肯定还存在不少缺点和不足，希望大家多多给予批评指正。

这本生态摄影集的出版，得到了国家林业局治沙办、宣传中心给予的大力支持和帮助，得到了阿拉善SEE基金会给予的资金方面的有力支撑。尤其是国家林业局张建龙局长、中国科学院李文华院士专门为本书作了序，治沙办潘迎珍主任、贾晓霞副主任、林琼处长，宣传中心程红主任、李天送副主任，保护司安立丹处长等领导同志给予了大力的支持和宝贵的建议。中国林业科学院荒漠化研究所卢琦所长，冯益明、马强、崔向慧等研究人员在业务方面给予了资料的提供和精心的指导。江西省林业科学院动物研究所所长黄晓凤以及王静等专业人员给予了很多帮助。另外，在资料收集和考察中，得到了各省（自治区、直辖市）林业、野生动植物保护、治沙等主管部门以及自然保护区、沙漠公园等一线工作同志的热情关照，还有为本书编辑出版付出辛苦努力的肖静、田红、黄华强、曹来等编辑，我在此一并表示衷心的感谢！没有他们的热情支持和帮助，仅凭我个人之力，这本书是无法按时顺利出版的。

陈建伟
2017年7月

Preface

Diverse Deserts of China is eventually ready for publication. Compared with the other two books, *Diverse Forests of China* and *Diverse Wetlands of China* that I had previously published under this series, this one has been relatively much tougher in preparation. For one thing, I have been subjected to very tight schedule, given that I would like to dedicate it to the COP 13 of the United Nations Convention to Combat Desertification, which means it will have to be made available before the conference. For the other, findings from previous studies concerning desert eco-systems that are available for my consultation are rather limited. For instance, the very issue concerning the geographical zoning of deserts in China has constantly remained a highly tricky point for me up to the moment when the present draft was about to be handed into to my editor for publication. Site observations, paperwork, double-checking second-hand information, consulting specialists in this field and so on, there are so many things that I have had to go through. Being the founder of China Desert Monitoring Center who personally initiated and organized the first national inventory of the country's deserts and who has later continually engaged in monitoring, researching and supervising works relevant with China's forests, wetlands, deserts as well as wildlife, I have over the past decades been to many remote, and even uninhabited deserts across the country and recorded my experiences with cameras. The breathtaking, or occasionally heartbreaking, pictures that I have taken over the years, plus the supportive hands and heart-warming encouragements from all my friends and colleagues, make up an inexhaustible source from which I draw heavily on for this eco-album.

If the forest ecosystems are to be compared to the lungs of the Earth whose primary function are to provide us with fresh air and oxygen, and the wetland ecosystems to its kidneys responsible for cleaning and purifying waters, it would make sense for us to compare the desert ecosystems to its spleens, which are the starting points of air and blood circulations within human bodies and, similarly, responsible for decomposition, filtering and providing primary forms of soil in the natural systems of the planet. Rather than being merely bleak and barren places, deserts in China present us with a rich variety of fantastic natural landscape wonders, including Yardangs, Gobis, deserts, desert grasslands, forests of soil, sandy lakes, salt pools, continental rivers, ancient castles and the silk roads, oasis and *etc*. Besides, they are also home to abundant wild fauna and flora, and microbial resources, most of which are among the finest species that had over long history survived the severe tests of natural selection and therefore have developed most favorable genes for sustaining themselves. Moreover, some species are precious and endemic to Chinese deserts. All these wildlife species and the environment in which they inhabit, in combination, constitute a special natural desert ecological system of the country, playing an irreplaceable role in nature ecology and biodiversity.

As a consequence of our poor understandings about this particular type of natural landscape, what deserts bring to people's minds are often such sorrowful images of sandstorms, farmhouses and crops buried beneath layer upon layer of sands, or refugees fleeing from impending sands. In addition, as they are typically associated with such daunting environments as severe droughts, infertile lands and remote settings, deserts are often taken as forbidden zones on this planet, the very mentioning of whose name would send people shudder with fear. Desertification is even compared to "cancer of the Earth". To put in short, desert ecosystems are ones for which we human beings bear the greatest fears, and the least yet most incorrect understanding. Approaches we adopt in addressing the relationship between deserts and human have often been characterized by mistaken beliefs that occasionally label them as something that we should stay away from as much as possible, or alternatively identifying them as enemies that we need to conquer at whatever costs. A root cause for these mistaken beliefs is that, rather than taking deserts as an integrated ecosystem, we tend to merely take them as mutually-isolated individual existences in the natural world. Desert ecosystems provide us with multiple ecological services, like sand fixation, soil conservation, water resources regulation, biodiversity conservation, rudimentary soil making, as well as global environment enhancement with sand dust. For better protection of these precious resources and better conservation of such ecosystems, a huge batch of nature reserves of desert ecosystem type have been established in China, take for instance, the world-renowned Shapotou Nature Reserve in Ningxia, and some others that boast vast stretch of lands as well as rich desert wildlife resources, such as the Qiangtang, Qomolangma Mountain reserves in Tibet, the Kekexili and Qinghai Lake reserves in Qinghai Province, the Cara Mak, Altun Mountain and

Lop Nor reserves in Xinjiang, the Ejin reserves in Inner Mongolia, the Akesai Reserve in Gansu Province, and the West Lake Reserve, to name just a few. Though less in number than forest and wetlands reserves, desert type nature reserves in China cover the largest sizes, accounting for approximately 5% of the country's total land territory.

However, desert ecosystems are very vulnerable, and once destroyed, it would be very hard for them to recover. Overuse of lands in arid, semi-arid and semi-humid regions is liable to result in land degradation, or in serious cases, in desertification, which refers to the deterioration or total loss of eco-services provided by deserts. The prevention of desertification means to contain the spread of human-inflicted deterioration and loss of desert eco-services, and in turn to recover those that have deteriorated or lost. Without a sound scientific recognition of the desert ecosystem, it would be hardly possible for us to come up with either proper approaches or effective methods in combating desertification. This issue will be repeatedly discussed in each chapter of the present album, and a special section at the end of the book is also devoted to an in-depth reflection on the human-desert relationship. The COP 13 of the United Nations Convention to Combat Desertification will soon be taking place in China in 2017, Which affirms the remarkable progresses that China has made over the years in combating desertification. This book will be dedicated to the Convention. For sure, due to limits of my own knowledge, mistakes and insufficiencies will inevitably exist in the book concerning understandings about desert ecosystems. Comments and constructive advices from readers will be highly appreciated.

I owe greatly, for the publication of this eco-album, to the keen supports afforded to me by the National Bureau of Desertification Combating (NBDC) and the Publicity Center of the State Forestry Administration (SFA), and to the generous funding provided by SEE Foundation. My earnest gratitude also goes to Mr. Zhang Jianlong, Minister of SFA and Mr. Li Wenhua, Academician of Chinese Academy of Sciences who kindly write prefaces for this book; Director General Pan Yingzhen, Deputy Director General Jia Xiaoxia, and Director Lin Qiong from the NBDC; Director General Cheng Hong and Deputy Director General Li Tiansong from the Publicity Center; as well as Director An Lidan from the Department of Wildlife Conservation and Nature Reserve Management of the SFA. In addition, I would like to extend my acknowledgement to Mr. Lu Qi, Director of the Research Institute of Desertification Combating (RIDC) under Chinese Academy of Forestry (CAF), as well as his colleagues Dr. Feng Yiming, Dr. Ma Qiang, and Dr. Cui Xianghui who have generously offered their professional expertise. Director Huang Xiaofeng and Ms. Wang Jing from the Forestry and Wildlife Research Institute of Jiangxi Province have also provided me with enlightening technical consultations. Throughout the process of deskwork and field-trips in preparation for this book, corresponding provincial authorities for forestry, wildlife conservation, desertification combating, as well as staff work at nature reserves and desert parks, have given me many much-appreciated helps. Last but not least, my heart-felt gratitude goes to those excellent editors of this book, including Xiao Jing, Tian Hong, Huang Huaqiang and Cao Lai, without whose diligent work and highly competent professional morale, publication of this book would undoubtedly be delayed.

CHEN JIANWEI
July 2017

目录 Contents

导言
Introduction ············ 28

1 松辽平原半湿润半干旱区
The Semi-humid and Semi-arid Areas in
the Songliao Plain ············ 36

2 内蒙古高原半干旱干旱区
The Semi-arid and Arid Areas in
the Inner Mongolia Plateau ············ 56

3 阿拉善高原与河西走廊干旱极干旱区
The Arid and Extremely Arid Areas in
the Alxa Plateau and the Hexi Corridor ············ 82

4 北疆盆地干旱极干旱区
The Arid and Extremely Arid Areas
in the Northern Xinjiang Basin ················ **116**

5 南疆盆地极干旱区
The Extremely Arid Areas
in the Southern Xinjiang Basin ················ **142**

6 青藏高原高寒干旱极干旱区
The Alpine Arid and Extremely Arid Areas
in the Qinghai-Tibet Plateau ················ **162**

生态思考
Ecological Reflections ················ *198*

物种简介
Introduction of Species ················ *212*

导言

荒漠生态系统和森林、湿地、海洋生态系统一样，是地球上最重要的自然生态系统之一，共同维系着包括人类在内地球万千生物的世代繁衍和整个地球生物圈的生态平衡。荒漠生态系统有如防风固沙、土壤保育、水资源调控、生物多样性保护、初级土壤制造、沙尘全球环境增益等生态功能。而荒漠因为干旱、荒芜、空旷且环境严酷，往往被人畏而远之，被视为生命禁区；更因为沙尘暴危害、沙化土地侵蚀而遭人诟病，并被视为"地球的癌症"。因此可以说，荒漠生态系统是一个人们最陌生、最畏惧、最不能正确认识的地球生态系统。

其实，荒漠生态系统分布于除南极洲外的地球各大洲，占到地球陆地面积的12%，是地球千万年延续下来的、不以人们主观意志为转移的客观存在，是地球生物基因库中不可或缺的荒漠生物基因库。荒漠生态系统是中国陆地生态系统最重要的组成部分之一，更是我国西北地区最主要的生态系统，其间蕴藏着大量珍稀、特有的野生动植物资源，是一类不可替代的、与整体自然生态环境休戚相关的独特生态系统。

荒漠生态系统

荒漠的基质依组成物质颗粒的大小而有石质、砾质和沙质荒漠之分。人们习惯将石质、砾质的荒漠称为戈壁，将沙质荒漠称为沙漠，也将较湿润、地下水位较高、植物生长较茂盛的沙漠称为沙地，草场退化就很容易形成沙地。另外，在长期干旱条件下，河湖沉积，泥沙表面干燥龟裂，植被稀少的称为泥漠，而泥漠水分蒸发后，盐分大量聚集于地表的，称为盐漠。

中国的戈壁、沙漠和沙地主要发生在温带、暖温带的极干旱、干旱、半干旱及半湿润地区，也发生在温带高寒干旱地区。戈壁、沙漠和沙地是只限于特定自然地带内才能发生的景观，都是非地带性景观。由于温度条件的差异，更由于湿润条件和基质的差异，不同区域的戈壁、沙漠和沙地在类型、程度上有很大差异，植被及再生能力以及抗风蚀、水蚀的能力也大相径庭，所赋含的资源状况及生态环境承载力也会有很大不同。

中国的戈壁划分为岩漠、砾漠两类，石质荒漠为岩漠，砾质荒漠为砾漠。岩漠一般覆盖在盆地的盆边或者山麓地带，如马鬃山、雅布赖山、贺兰山、罕乌拉山、巴彦乌拉山的山前，喜马拉雅山脉北麓等。砾漠一般容易分布在岩漠低处或者在如巴丹吉林、腾格里、乌兰布和沙漠的沙漠外围等。

中国的八大沙漠包括位于新疆南部塔里木盆地中心的塔克拉玛干沙漠，新疆北部准噶尔盆地中央的古尔班通古特沙漠，内蒙古阿拉善右旗北部的巴丹吉林沙漠，内蒙古阿拉善左旗西南部和甘肃中部的腾格里沙漠，青海柴达木盆地腹地的柴达木沙漠，新疆东部、甘肃西部的库姆塔格沙漠，内蒙古鄂尔多斯高原北部的库布齐沙漠和内蒙古西部、宁夏东部的乌兰布和沙漠。

中国的四大沙地包括位于大兴安岭和冀北山地之间三角地带的科尔沁沙地，横跨内蒙古、宁夏和陕西的毛乌素沙地，位于内蒙古锡林郭勒高原中部的浑善达克沙地和内蒙古东北部呼伦贝尔高原的呼伦贝尔沙地。除了八大沙漠、四大沙地以外，中国还广泛分布一些相比规模较小的零星沙漠、沙地。中国的戈壁、沙漠和沙地的总面积共约160万 km^2。

荒漠生态系统是以旱生、超旱生的草本、小乔木、灌木和半灌木占优势的生物群落与赖以生存的动物、微生物及其环境所组成的综合体，有普氏野马、藏羚羊、野牦牛、隼、大鸨等上百种珍稀野生动物，还有很多具有特殊的食用、药用、特用价值的珍稀植物，如甘草、锁阳、肉苁蓉、罗布麻等；有很多植物如禾本科、豆科、柽柳科、莎草科、杞柳、锦葵科、鸢尾科的植物是食品、饲料、制药等工业的重要原料，也有一些耐旱的乔木如胡杨、榆、沙地云杉、沙枣、沙地樟子松等。在其生境中，众多物种之间相互依存、相互制约和有机统一，在复杂的食物链中各司其职，维护着荒漠生态系统的平衡，共同构成了一个和谐共生的整体。但是，也因为这个系统的特别脆弱性，在自然条件变化和人为的干扰下，荒漠生态系统尤其容易受到破坏、甚至崩塌，给其他生态系统带来严重危害，给人类带来的伤害同样也是巨大的。这就是我们人类必须要认真地、正确地认识荒漠生态系统本质的根本原因。

和森林的端庄、湿地的秀美相比，荒漠是粗犷的。与森林、湿地不容荒漠相比，荒漠待森林、湿地却更有胸怀。水多时，荒漠将洼处让给湿地，广揽湿地入怀，将水热条件最好的地方给了乔木、灌木，容许林木自强；水少时，它或安静如处，或独自徘徊；脾气不好时，也如脱缰野马随风施暴、让人类的家园处处充满尘埃。因此，我们"看"荒漠，不仅要多方位、多角度地看，更要从是一个地球不可或缺的生态系统的角度来看；不能"只看荒芜野旷，不看生命生长；只知荒漠危害，不知荒漠胸怀"。

荒漠生物多样性

荒漠植物是荒漠生态系统的重要组成部分，在极端严酷的环境条件下，通过长期的适应和进化，逐渐形成了许多特异的生态适应机制，在收集、储存或减少水分消耗等方面形成了独特的形态特征或生理特征。例如，叶面角质层加厚，叶片肉质化而能储存水分或者叶片富含盐分、泌盐等，小叶、少叶、无叶而以绿色枝条或茎秆进行光合作用，发达的根系便于吸取地下深层的水分等特征。这些旱生、超旱生的草本、灌木和半灌木、小乔木形成了荒漠植被群落。荒漠植物不仅是荒漠生态系统的生产者，而且在防风固沙、土壤保育、维护生物多样性、改善环境方面有着多种极其重要的功能。

作为消费者的荒漠动物也有着很多特性，诸如，都能耐干旱、耐寒冷，适应日温差大的气温，毛色浅淡或黄褐色，少鲜明的色彩和斑纹，动物种类较少，尤其是喜好湿润的两栖爬行动物少等特点。这里最具代表性的动物是有蹄类动物，如野骆驼、普氏野马、普氏原羚、藏羚羊、野牦牛等都是中国荒漠特有的或原生的动物，它们特别能够适应开阔的地带环境，为了寻找水源和适应食物变化的季节需要，均具有迅速奔跑的能力，常常集结成群、并做长距离迁徙。由于日温差大，许多动物有昼伏夜出的习性。狼、狐、鼬等食肉类动物和雕、鸳、鹰、隼等猛禽，主要依靠大量的啮齿类动物为生，有时也食小鸟等。而啮齿类动物是荒漠区广泛分布、数量众多的哺乳类动物，为适应严酷的环境，啮齿类动物均有高度的繁殖能力。鸟类也以适应荒漠环境为主要特征，除荒漠中湿地有迁徙鸟类生活外，秃鹫、兀鹫、胡兀鹫等食腐动物是荒漠的清洁工，以食动物尸体为主。大鸨、毛腿沙鸡等适应沙土中行走，角百灵、蒙古百灵等羽毛近似沙色，通常结群奔食。鸟鼠（兔）同穴、蛙鼠（兔）同穴的行为，更是草原、荒漠地带动物之间相互依存的特殊生态现象。

《联合国防治荒漠化公约》与荒漠化

《联合国防治荒漠化公约》（以下简称《公约》）是1992年里约环境发展大会《21世纪议程》框架下的三大重要国际环境公约之一。该公约于1996年12月正式生效，1997年中国正式加入，目前《公约》共有196个缔约方。《公约》的核心目标是由各国政府共同制定国家级、次区域级和区域级行动方案，并与捐助方、地方社区和非政府组织合作，以对抗应对荒漠化的挑战。《公约》对于荒漠化的定义是"指包括气候变异和人类活动在内的种种因素造成的干旱、半干旱和亚湿润干旱区的土地退化"。而土地退化是指旱地的生物或经济生产力的下降或丧失，其含义应该包括草场退化、生物多样性破坏、物种消亡、水土流失、土地沙化、盐渍化、沙丘活化、沙丘入侵等以某一环境因素为标志的具体的自然生态环境退化过程。干旱、半干旱和半湿润干旱区的森林、草原、湿地被严重破坏，都可能形成沙地、沙漠。

中国加入《公约》和对《公约》的认真履行，使我国保护荒漠生态系统、防沙治沙、防治荒漠化的工作在原来的基础上提升到了一个更为重要的高度。按照《公约》的标尺，结合中国的具体情况，走上了全国范围内的荒漠生态系统保护以及荒漠化、沙化土地（由于各种因素形成的地表呈现以沙物质为主要标志，植被破坏、沙土裸露的退化土地）的调查、监测与科学防治的快车道上来。

我国荒漠化、沙化土地的分布范围相当广阔，西起新疆，东至黑龙江，北到内蒙古，南至青藏高原，断续展布于我国北部、西部的干旱、半干旱及半湿润地区，主要分布在毛乌素、浑善达克、科尔沁、呼伦贝尔等沙地及其周围的草场、旱地等。二十世纪五六十年代，我国沙化土地每年以 1560 km² 速度扩展，八十年代以每年 2100 km² 速度扩展，九十年代初期每年以 2460 km² 速度扩展，九十年代后期每年扩展达 3436 km²。截至 1999 年，我国有荒漠化土地 267.4 万 km²，占国土总面积的 27.9%；全国沙化土地总面积为 174.31 万 km²，占国土总面积的 18.2%。根据 2002 年第二次全国荒漠化、沙化土地监测结果：我国土地荒漠化、沙化呈局部好转、整体恶化之势。

荒漠生态地理区划

由于人们长期对于荒漠生态系统的不了解、不重视，我国目前还没有颁布过权威统一的荒漠生态系统自然地理区划。近些年来，由于荒漠对于人类生产生活的危害侵蚀，扬尘、沙尘暴等对于环境的严重威胁，荒漠化土地的不断扩展，国家对于荒漠现状及发展趋势给予了

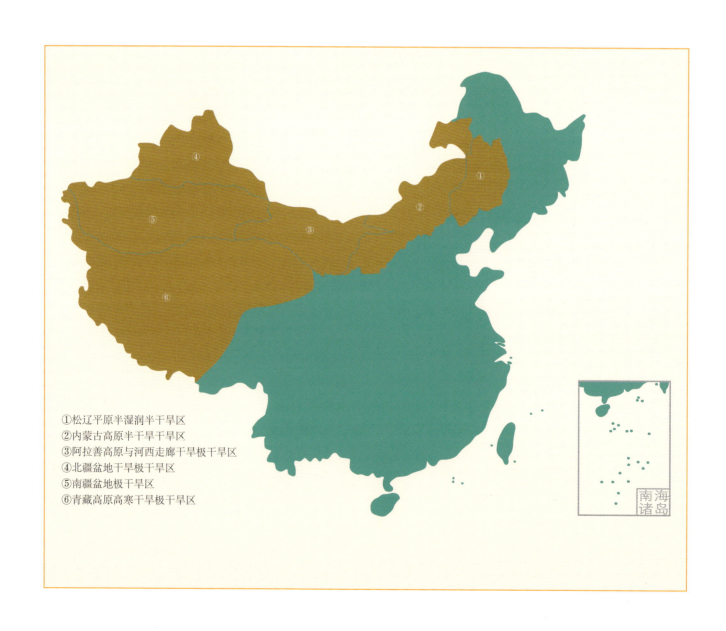

① 松辽平原半湿润半干旱区
② 内蒙古高原半干旱干旱区
③ 阿拉善高原与河西走廊干旱极干旱区
④ 北疆盆地干旱极干旱区
⑤ 南疆盆地极干旱区
⑥ 青藏高原高寒干旱极干旱区

越来越多的关注。《公约》在中国的履约实施，国家对于荒漠生态系统及其野生动植物保护的强化，使得不少科学家在原来研究的基础上做了深入的探讨。本书从郑度院士的生态地理区划出发，参考申元村、卢琦等专家对中国沙漠、戈壁生态地理区划分成八个区的研究成果，为了更加符合科普和宣传的客观需要，经过整理合并，将中国的荒漠区划为六个部分，并将南界推到了喜马拉雅山脉北麓，六个部分区划如下：①松辽平原半湿润半干旱区；②内蒙古高原半干旱干旱区；③阿拉善高原与河西走廊干旱极干旱区；④北疆盆地干旱极干旱区；⑤南疆盆地极干旱区；⑥青藏高原高寒干旱极干旱区。这里需要提出的是，青藏高原唐古拉山以南以及喜马拉雅山脉北麓、昆仑山腹地、羌塘等地不仅高寒，更是干旱、极干旱气候，尽管因为冰雪融水湖泊众多，但地质年代年轻脆弱，在干旱、极干旱条件下产生了大量的戈壁、沙漠，如喜马拉雅山脉北麓、昆仑山腹地的大量戈壁，世界上海拔最高的沙漠——库木库里沙漠，喜马拉雅山脉北麓、雅鲁藏布江上中游处处可见的戈壁、流动沙丘等，更有高寒荒漠植物群落及藏羚羊、野牦牛、盘羊、高山兀鹫等荒漠特有动物在这里自由自在地生长。我们以前在进行中国生态系统划分的时候，往往把青藏高原统归为草原生态系统，其实是不完全的，青藏高原所具有的特殊的高寒荒漠生态系统不应被遗漏。

由于篇幅有限，本书在编辑中对于分布比较广的荒漠景观、动植物广布种，采取了相对集中在一章里面展示，其余区域就尽量不再重复出现的办法。例如，各种沙丘类型，因为南疆比较集中、多样，又比较典型，所以就主要集中在此章论述，在其余章节里只是点到。库姆塔格沙漠位于塔里木盆地的东缘，地跨甘肃和新疆两省，但大部分在新疆，还因为它和塔克拉玛干沙漠类似，都是处于极干旱区的流动沙漠，因此将库姆塔格沙漠主要列入第五章论述等。

需要强调的是，由于荒漠生态系统的脆弱性，以及人与荒漠之间总是不断纠缠在沙进人退或人进沙退，土地或退化、或进化（恢复）的局面之中，尽管本书的主旨讲的是荒漠、荒漠生态系统本身，但是也必须要讲到荒漠化。荒漠是一种现象，荒漠化是一种过程——土地的退化过程。荒漠化不仅在本书最后专门列出生态思考部分讲，在每章中也要就该区荒漠化的威胁、荒漠化的治理、人与自然的关系做出论述。本书每章章前小图及里面的内容大致也是按照大、中景观，戈壁沙漠沙地，植物动物，人与自然关系的逻辑顺序排列的。

荒漠化的"防"与"治"

既然荒漠化就是土地的退化，因此，防治荒漠化必须要"防止"与"治理"双管齐下，"坚持保护优先，自然恢复为主"。防止土地退化的前提是要充分尊重自然、认识荒漠生态系统的内在规律及其重要价值，坚持保护优先，才能保护好现有的荒漠生态系统，应该在典型、集中、有代表性的荒漠地区根据不同情况划建自然保护区、野生动物植物保护地、荒漠公园等，划定并严守沙区生态红线，采取封沙、封滩、禁牧、禁垦的办法防止土地的沙化、退化，不断扩大封禁保护的面积，建立和完善荒漠区土地封禁制度。禁止和最大程度减少人为活动，避免干扰、伤害荒漠野生动植物和破坏荒漠生态系统的平衡，充分发挥生态系统自我恢复的功能，实现人与自然和谐相处。而治理土地退化就是要"师法自然"，宜林则林、宜草则草，因地制宜选择绿化模式，科学地人工干预已经退化的土地，因地制宜、分区施策，完善沙化土地修复机制等，不断扩大修复面积，不断提升防沙治沙科技创新水平。通过工程治理、生态保护补偿、鼓励多元化投入等政策措施，加快治理的步伐和水平。

和已经出版的"一滴水生态摄影丛书"系列之《多样性的中国森林》《多样性的中国湿地》一样，《多样性的中国荒漠》同样是致力于用精美的图文并茂的形式将中国最重要的陆地生态系统科学、生动、直观地呈现给大家，以达到宣传、帮助大家更好地认识并保护这些生态系统的目的。由于荒漠生态系统的脆弱性和中国这些年在防治荒漠化方面取得的举世瞩目的成就，本书还特别加重了生态思考部分的篇幅和分量，以迎接"《联合国防治荒漠化公约》第十三次缔约方大会"2017年在中国的召开。

Introduction

Desert ecosystem, the same as forest, wetland and marine ecosystems, is one of the most important natural ecosystems on the Earth. These ecosystems together sustain the reproduction of millions of living creatures, including human beings, and the ecological balance of the entire earth biosphere. Desert ecosystems provide us with multiple ecological services, like sand fixation, soil conservation, water resources regulation, biodiversity conservation, rudimentary soil making, as well as global environment enhancement with sand dust. However, deserts, because of the drought, barrenness, emptiness and harsh environment that they are typically associated with, are often taken out of our ignorance as the "forbidden zones of life". To make it worse, they are frequently blamed for causing sand and dust storms, land erosions and consequently compared to "the cancer of the earth". For these reasons, it is not exaggeration for us to conclude that desert ecosystems are the scariest, the strangest ones among this Planet's entire ecosystems about which we still have the poorest understanding.

In fact, desert ecosystems are found on almost all continents except the Antarctica, accounting for 12% of the earth's land area. They are the physical existence of the earth for thousands of years, a fact that is not subject to changes by human beings' wills. As one of the most important part of terrestrial ecosystems in China, desert ecosystem is also the most important ecosystem in Northwest China, which contains a large number of rare and endemic wildlife resources, and makes up the indispensable desert biological gene pools, which in turn is integral part of the Earth's biological gene pool. Meanwhile, it is also a kind of irreplaceable and unique ecosystems closely related to the whole natural ecological environment.

Desert Ecosystem

According to the size of the matrix particles, deserts can be divided into stony, gravelly or sandy deserts. People generally refer to stony and gravelly deserts as Gobi, and sandy desert as desert. Besides, deserts that are relatively wetter and have higher groundwater levels and where plants flourish are normally known as sandy lands. Degraded grasslands are highly liable to be turned into sandy lands. In addition, rivers and lakes become mud deserts when subject to long periods of drought that leaves the sediment surfaces dry, cracked and sparsely covered with vegetation. In cases when water evaporation in mud deserts leaves huge quantity of salt deposits to accumulate over the land, salt deserts would come into being.

China's Gobis, deserts and sandy lands are primarily found in the extremely arid, arid, semi-arid and semi-humid areas of the temperate and warm temperate zones, as well as in the temperate alpine areas. Gobis, deserts, and sandy lands are landscapes that come into being only under specific natural conditions, featuring azonality. Due to the differences in their respective temperature, together with huge variations in moisture contents, Gobis, deserts and sandy lands in different geographical regions may differ greatly in their types, and scopes, so do their corresponding vegetation and its regeneration capacity, and tolerance against wind or water erosion. Sharp deviations might also exist in their resources endowments and carrying capacities.

Gobis in China can be divided, depending on the size of their surface substances, into rocky deserts and gravel deserts. Rocky deserts are usually found in the margin of basins or at foothills, with the Mazong Mountain, the Yabrai Hill, the Helan Mountain, the Hanwula Mountain, the piedmont of Bayanwula Mountain and *etc*. as typical examples. Gravel deserts are generally found in the lower rocky deserts or the periphery of some deserts, such as the Badan Jaran Desert, the Tengger Desert, and the Ulan Buh Desert.

The eight major deserts in China are as follows: the Taklimakan Desert (located in central Tarim Basin, southern Xinjiang), the Gurbantunggut Desert (in central Junggar Basin, northern Xinjiang), the Badan Jaran Desert (in northern Alxa Right Banner, Inner Mongolia), the Tengger Desert (between the southwest of Alxa Left Banner of Inner Mongolia and central Gansu Province), the Qaidam Desert (in the hinterland of Qaidam Basin, Qinghai), the Kumtag Desert (in the eastern part of Xinjiang and the western part of Gansu), the Kubuqi Desert (in northern Ordos Plateau, Inner Mongolia) and the Ulan Buh Desert (in eastern Ningxia).

The four major sandy lands in China include: the Horqin Sandy Land (located in the triangular area between the Da Hinggan Mountains and northern Hebei mountainous area), the Maowusu Sandy Land (ranging across Inner Mongolia, Ningxia and Shaanxi), the Hunshandake Sandy Land (in central Xilingol Plateau, Inner Mongolia) and the Hulunbuir Sandy Land (in Hulunbuir Plateau, Northeastern Inner Mongolia). Apart from the eight major deserts and the four major sandy lands, China is also extensively dotted with some relative smaller deserts and sandy lands. The total area of Gobis, deserts and sandy lands in China is about 1.6 million km^2.

Desert ecosystems refer to integrated settings that typically include bio-communities composed primarily of drought-resistant or super drought-resistant grasses, small trees and shrubs, and wildlife and microbes that rely on such bio-communities. Representative wildlife species inhabiting these systems are as follows: over 100 rare and precious wild fauna species that include *Equus ferus* ssp. *Przewalskii*, tibetan antelopes, wild yaks, falcos, *Otis tarda* and *etc*.; rich variety of rare and precious wild flora applicable for both food and medicine that include *Glycyrrhiza uralensis*, *Cynomorium songaricum*, *Cistanche deserticola*, *Apocynum* venetum and *etc*.; plenty of plant species under such families of Gramineae, Leguminosae sp., Tamaricaceae, Cyperaceae, *Salix integra*, Malvaceae and Iridaceae can be used as key raw materials of food, fodder or medicine; some drought-resistant arbor trees such as *Populus euphratica*, *Ulmus pumila*, *Picea mongolica*, *Elaeagnus angustifolia*, Mongolian Scotch Pine and *etc*. In their habitats, many species, mutually interdependent, mutually restrictive and organically united as a whole, perform their respective duties in the complex food chain, maintain the balance of the desert ecosystem, and constitute a harmonious symbiosis unity jointly. However, given that these systems are extremely vulnerable, they are highly susceptible to any slight changes induced either by nature or by human interference, even resulting in the total collapse of the entire ecological system and inflicting huge losses to human society. This explains why we human beings must conscientiously and correctly understand the nature of the desert ecosystems.

Different from the splendour of forests and the elegance of wetlands, deserts are characterized by their rudimentary forms and unmatchable strength. In sharp contrast to the dispelling attitudes held by forests and wetlands towards deserts, the latter often appear to be more tolerant and inclusive towards the former ones. In water-abundant seasons, deserts will give up their low-lying parts to wetlands and allow space for their expansion, creating favorable water and heat conditions for trees, shrubs to take roots and flourish. In water-deficit seasons, deserts will quietly take back into its embrace lands over which vegetation used to thrive in water-rich periods. Sure, they might in moments of ill temper behavior badly and rampage through our homelands like wild horses, causing damages to properties as well as human lives. But nevertheless, multi-faceted and multi-dimensional views should be taken in the evaluation of deserts. Rather than the partial and one-sided viewpoint that focuses only on the ruthless, detrimental impacts and neglects the tolerant, beneficial influences that they bring to human beings, a more holistic view should be adopted that take deserts as indispensable parts of the overall ecosystem of this Planet.

Desert Biodiversity

As an important part of the desert ecosystem, desert plants have adapted in the long process of evolution to the extremely harsh conditions typical of such landscape, and consequently developed distinctive morphological or physiological mechanisms for acquiring, storing water and cutting down on water consumption. For example, foliage stratum corneum thickens and leaves become succulent to store moisture; leaves become rich in salt and ooze salts; plants have small leaves, little leaves or even no leaves and photosynthesize with green shoots or stems; plants possess well-developed roots to absorb moisture from the deep underground. These unique features enable the xerophytic, super-xerophytic herbs, small arbors, shrubs and semi-shrubs to make up the desert biome. Desert plants are not only the primary producers of desert ecosystems, but also play critical roles in wind breaking, sand fixation, soil conservation, biodiversity maintaining and environmental improvement.

Desert animals, as consumers, and secondary producers as well, of desert ecosystems, have also developed characteristics conducive to their survival under the harsh conditions of deserts. For example, they have the ability to adapt to drought, cold, and huge day-night temperature variation; their hair colors are light or yellowish brown and have less bright colors and markings; and there are fewer species of animals, especially those amphibians and reptiles that prefer wetness. The most representative animals here are ungulate animals, such as wild camels, *Equus przewalskii*, *Procapra przewalskii*, Tibetan antelopes, wild yaks, *etc*., all of which belong to indigenous species that are unique to deserts in China. They are particularly capable of adapting to the open and wide environment. In order to find water and to adapt to seasonal changes in needs for food, they all have the ability to run quickly, and often gather in groups and migrate over long distances. Because of the large temperature difference between day and night, many animals have nocturnal habits. Wolves, foxes, skunks and other carnivores and vultures, buzzards, eagles, falcons and other birds of prey, mainly rely on a large number of rodents, and occasionally on smaller birds, for survival. Meanwhile, rodents, mammals that abound in vast stretches of deserts, have also developed remarkable fertilities to cope with the harsh environment in which they live. Birds are also equipped with features suitable for survival in desert environment. Besides some migratory birds that regularly visit wetlands in deserts, cinereous vultures, condors and lammergeiers and other scavengers that live on carcasses of animals also abound in deserts. Some birds like great bustards and *Syrrhaptes paradoxus* are used to walking in the sands, and other birds such as horned larks and Mongolian larks with feathers that are similar to sand colors are used to living in flocks for forage. The phenomena that birds and mice (rabbits) share the same cave, or alternatively frogs and rats (rabbits) share the same cave, are telling examples of the unique, mutually dependent relationship among animals inhabiting the grassland and desert areas.

The United Nations Convention to Combat Desertification and the Desertification

The United Nations Convention to Combat Desertification (hereinafter referred to as the Convention) is one of the three major international environmental conventions under the framework of "the 21st Century Agenda" adopted at Rio Environmental Development Conference in 1992. The Convention entered into force in December 1996 and China formally joined it in 1997. At present, there are 196 signatory parties to the Convention. The core target of the Convention is that governments work together to develop national, subregional and regional action programs and to work with donors, local communities and non-governmental organizations to combat the challenges of addressing desertification. The Convention defines desertification as "land degradation in arid, semi-arid and sub-humid arid areas caused by various factors including climate variability and human activities". Land degradation refers to the decline or loss of biological or economic productivity in dry lands. It should include some specific processes of natural ecological degradation marked by an environmental factor, for example, grassland degradation, destruction of biodiversity, species extinction, soil erosion, land desertification, salinization, dune activation, dune invasion and so on. Forests, grasslands and wetlands in arid, semi-arid and arid and sub-humid regions, when subjected to serious destructions, are all liable to be degraded to sandy lands or deserts.

China's earnest implementation of the Convention has improved our country's efforts in protecting desert ecosystems, preventing and combating desertification to a higher level. In accordance with the standards of the Convention and specific conditions of China, we have embarked on a new roadway to implementing nationwide conservation of desert ecosystems and carrying on investigation, monitoring and scientific control over desertified and sandified lands (a type of lands on which, due to the influence of various reasons, soil was degraded, vegetation was destroyed, and sandy soil was exposed bare).

Desertification and desertified lands are found over vast areas in China. From Xinjiang in the west to Heilongjiang in the east, they dot intermittently across the extensive stretch of arid, semi-arid and semi humid areas in northern China, with Maowusu, Hunshandake, Horqin and Hulunbuir and their surrounding grasslands and dry lands as major examples. Over the last five decades in the last century, land degradation in China had been developing at increasingly faster paces, with deserts expanding at alarming annual rates: 1560 km^2 in the 1950s and 1960s, 2100 km^2 in the 1980s, 2460 km^2 in early 1990s, and 3436 km^2 in late 1990s. According to the second national survey of desertification and sandified lands carried out in 2002, in spite of the improvement in certain local areas, the overall situation deteriorated. As of 1999, China had 2.674 million km^2 of deserts, accounting for 27.9% of the country's total land area, and the total area of sandified lands was 1.7431 million km^2, accounting for 18.2% of the total land area of China.

Geographical Zoning of Desert Ecosystem

Because of poor understanding and insufficient attention over the past to desert ecosystem, there is not yet any authoritative and uniformed system available in China for zoning the natural desert ecosystem of the country. Over

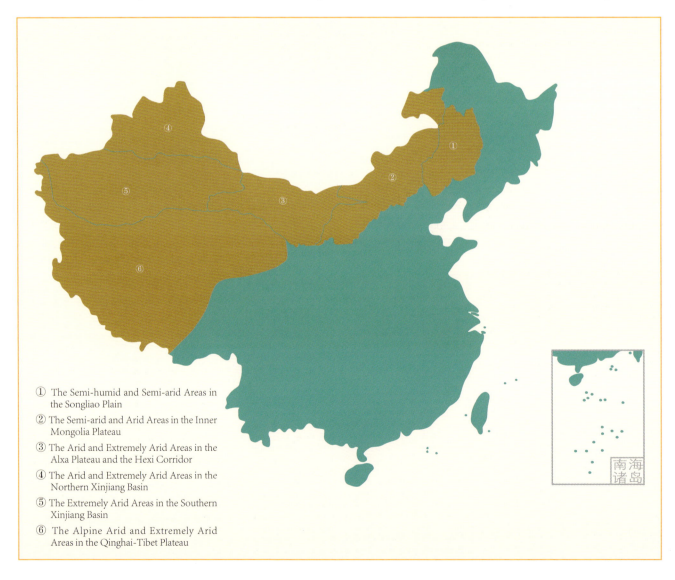

① The Semi-humid and Semi-arid Areas in the Songliao Plain
② The Semi-arid and Arid Areas in the Inner Mongolia Plateau
③ The Arid and Extremely Arid Areas in the Alxa Plateau and the Hexi Corridor
④ The Arid and Extremely Arid Areas in the Northern Xinjiang Basin
⑤ The Extremely Arid Areas in the Southern Xinjiang Basin
⑥ The Alpine Arid and Extremely Arid Areas in the Qinghai-Tibet Plateau

the years, human production and livelihood are badly eroded by desertification, our environment is seriously threatened by flying dust and dust storms, and the land desertification is expanding. This worsening situation has urged the Chinese government to pay more attention to the current situation. With the implementation of the *United Nations Convention to Combat Desertification* in China, and with the heightened endeavors of the State to address the issue, scientists are dedicating increasing efforts to protect desert ecosystems and wildlife inhabiting them. In this book, we shall, following the approaches proposed by academician Zheng Du, and bearing in mind the results yielded from studies of Shen Yuancun, Lu Qi and other experts concerning desert ecosystem zoning, divide China's deserts into six zones: (a) The Semi-humid and Semi-arid Areas in the Songliao Plain; (b) The Semi-arid and Arid Areas in the Inner Mongolia Plateau; (c) The Arid and Extremely Arid Areas in the Alxa Plateau and the Hexi Corridor; (d) The Arid and Extremely Arid Areas in the Northern Xinjiang Basin; (e) The Extremely Arid Areas in the Southern Xinjiang Basin; (f) The Alpine Arid and Extremely Arid Areas in the Qinghai-Tibet Plateau. It should be pointed out that certain regions in the Qinghai-Tibet Plateau, such as the extremely cold and dry or super-dry areas lying between the south of Tang-ku-la Mountains and the north slope of the Himalayas, the hinterlands of Kunlun Mountains, and Qiangtang area where the geographical conditions are highly vulnerable, also have vast areas of Gobis and deserts, even though lakes formed by melted snow and ice abound in these regions. Take for instance, Gobis, shifting sand dunes can be readily found in the north of the Himalayas, in the hinterlands of Kunlun Mountains, and in the middle and upper reaches of the Yarlung Zangbo River, the Kumukuli Desert, the highest one in the world, being just such a case. These areas are also home to some super cold-resistant desert plant communities and endemic desert wildlife species such as Tibetan antelopes, wild yaks, argals and Himalayan vultures. We have traditionally put the Qinghai-Tibet Plateau holistically under the category of grassland ecosystems, which is somehow not completely correct, for the unique frigid desert ecosystems existing there were not given due consideration.

Given the limited space available, certain types of desert landscapes and corresponding fauna, floral species that exist over vast geographical areas will be covered only within one chapter that is dedicated specially to the region where a specific type exist in concentration. For example, because dunes in southern Xinjiang are numerous in quantity, rich in variety, and representative in their respective categories, they are introduced in-depth only in the chapter devoted to this region, and only briefly touched upon in other places if needed. Take for another example, the Kumtag Desert is located on the eastern edge of the Tarim Basin, covering parts of both Gansu and Xinjiang, but since it lies mostly in Xinjiang and is similar in nature to the Taklimakan Desert, both being shifting deserts in extremely arid area, it is mainly elaborated on in the chapter themed on the Zone mentioned above, namely, the Extremely Arid Areas in the Southern Xinjiang Basin.

It is worth noting that due to the fragility of desert ecosystems, the relationship between human beings and deserts are constantly changing, with either human beings or deserts taking the upper hand for a given period of time. Although the central theme of this book is about deserts and desert ecosystems, it is inevitable to touch upon the idea of desertification, which is not only addressed in the part of Ecological Reflections at the end of the book, but also elaborated on in other chapters when the relationship between human and nature, threats imposed by desertification are dealt with. Deserts are a sort of objective existence, whereas desertification is a process-one of land degradation. The arrangement of contents in each pre-chapter small picture and each chapter follows the general logical order listed as follows: the macro-landscape; the medium-scaled landscape; Gobi desert and sandy lands; desert plants and animals; the relationship between human beings and nature.

The "Prevention" and "Control" of Desertification

Since desertification is the degradation of land, combating desertification must adopt the two-pronged strategy of "prevention" and "control", priority to conservation, and focus on natural recovery. A prerequisite for preventing land degradation is a thorough understanding about the inherent laws and crucial values of desert ecosystems, which in turn forms the foundation for respecting nature. Nature reserves, wildlife protected areas, desert parks must be set up in typical desert regions where various desert ecosystems concentrate, with strict bans placed on animal grazing and land cultivation in restrictive zones like sandy lands or sandy beaches. We ought to prohibit or reduce human activities to the greatest possible extent, and avoid intruding into or damaging desert wildlife and destroying the balance of desert ecosystems, hence continuously expanding the area of enclosure reserves, establishing and perfecting the system of land ban in desert areas. In our efforts to put land degradation under control, we need to "follow the inherent laws of nature" in dealing with the degraded land scientifically and through measures that fit the local conditions, with forests and grass vegetation duly established on suitable sites, so as to improve the restoration mechanism of degraded lands. We also need to continuously expand the repair areas and improve the scientific and technological innovation level in desertification prevention and control.Through such policy measures as engineering management, ecological protection compensation, and incentives for diversified investment, we can hopefully accelerate the pace in this regard.

Like *Diverse Forests of China* and *Diverse Wetlands of China* I have previously published under the A Single Drop of Water Ecological Photography Album Series, this *Diverse Deserts of China* is also committed to, through exquisite pictures and illustrations, to presenting to our readers knowledge concerning the critical terrestrial ecosystems in China in scientific, vivid and easily accessible manners, thus enhancing people's awareness about these ecosystems and mobilizing the interest of the whole society for conserving them. Given that desert ecosystems are often highly susceptible to adverse impacts, and to celebrate the remarkable progresses China has made over the years in combating desertification, additional weights have been placed on the *Ecological Reflections part* of the present book. The author would like to dedicate the book to the COP 13 of the United Nations Convention to Combat Desertification that will soon be taking place in China in 2017.

1

松辽平原
半湿润半干旱区
The Semi-humid and Semi-arid Areas in the Songliao Plain

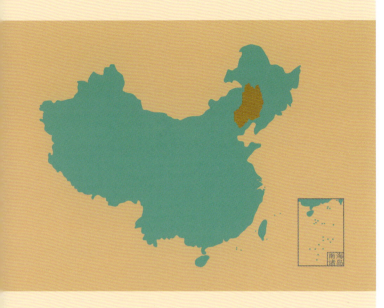

松辽平原半湿润半干旱区

　　该区域位于中国地势的第三级阶梯北部，也是该阶梯唯一的荒漠区。该区属大兴安岭东麓，松辽平原西部，分布范围北起齐齐哈尔市北侧，南至内蒙古巴林右旗—翁牛特旗—奈曼旗—库伦旗—辽宁彰武县章古台连线，东以黑龙江省杜尔伯特县东界—吉林省扶余县—双辽市—辽宁省康平县—彰武县连线为界，西为内蒙古科尔沁右翼中旗—阿鲁科尔沁旗连线。该地域中发育了科尔沁沙地和松嫩沙地等。

　　在中国荒漠区中，该区属温带半湿润半干旱区，生态环境条件最为优越，年均降水量200～400 mm，甚至可达500 mm，干燥度1.0～1.5。沙地绝大部分为固定半固定沙丘，高2～20 m不等，流沙呈小面积斑点状分布，流沙表层5 mm以下都有稳定的湿沙层。

　　科尔沁沙地、松嫩沙地植物生长良好，除草本及灌木外，还有乔木生长。榆树林是松辽平原沙地上发育的顶级植物群落，构成森林草原景观，对于维持区域生态平衡乃至东北草原区生态环境质量均具有重要作用。

　　在该区，由于降水条件好，西辽河及其支流流经科尔沁沙地，嫩江及其支流流经松嫩沙地，沙地中形成不少湿地、水泡子等，有不少水鸟在这里栖息，也有如白鹤、丹顶鹤、白枕鹤、蓑羽鹤等珍稀鸟类在春、秋两季迁徙途经停歇觅食、补充体力，因此这里成为世界著名的东亚—澳大利西亚水鸟迁徙路线上的关键地区。沙地中有沙蜥、沙鸡、黑琴鸡等生长繁衍。

　　相比较其他沙地，该地区水、热条件最佳，乔、灌、草都能生长，只要采取退耕还林还牧、封沙育草等措施，经过4～5年的努力，沙丘植被覆盖度就会大大增加，流沙就可以逐渐固定下来，荒漠化的发展趋势就可以得到有效抑制。因此，降低或杜绝草场开垦开矿、保护和改良草场、合理放牧限牧、增加植被防风固沙是本区资源合理利用与自然环境保护的主要任务，这对于维持区域生态平衡和生态环境质量均具有重要作用，也是使该区生态系统得到恢复和稳定的关键。

（前页）林草沙湿共同体·内蒙古科尔沁沙地
在中国六大荒漠区中，这里有别于其他区的特殊之处就是光、热、水条件最好，乔、灌、草都能生长，在大自然和人类的共同作用下，呈现出沙、水、林、草相互交织的景观。

(Previous Page) Community of Forest, Grassland, Sandy Land and Wetland—Horqin Sandy Land, Inner Mongolia
In China's six major desert areas, the Horqin Sandy Land owns a special feature that it has the best light, heat and water conditions, and trees, shrubs and grass can all grow well here. Thanks to the joint intervention of nature and human beings, a unique landscape composed alternately of sands, waters, forests and grassland has come into being.

（从左至右）
沙地景观·黑龙江松嫩沙地
玉龙沙湖·内蒙古赤峰
沙地榆树·内蒙古科尔沁沙地
蓑羽鹤示爱·内蒙古兴安盟
现代牧羊人·内蒙古通辽

(From Left to Right)
Sandy Landscape—Songnen Sandy Land, Heilongjiang
Yulong Sand Lake—Chifeng, Inner Mongolia
Sandy Elm Trees—Horqin Sandy Land, Inner Mongolia
Demoiselle Cranes in Love—Xing'an League, Inner Mongolia
The Modern Shepherd — Tongliao, Inner Mongolia

The Sem-humid and Semi-arid Areas in the Songliao Plain

As for its distribution range, from the north to the south, it starts from the north side of Qiqihar City to the line of Bahrain Right Banner, Ongniud Bannar, Naiman Banner, Hure Banner of Inner Mongolia and Zhanggutai of Zhangwu County of Liaoning; from the east to the west, it starts from the line of the eastern boundary of Durbat County of Heilongjiang, Fuyu County of Jilin, Shuangliao City, Kangping City of Liaoning and Zhangwu County to the line of Horqin Right Wing Middle Banner and Ar Horqin Banner of Inner Mongolia. Horqin Sandy Land, Songnen Sandy Land and other sandy lands are developed in this area.

This region belongs to the temperate semi-humid and semi-arid area. In this area, with the average annual rainfall of 200-400 mm, or even up to 500 mm and the aridity of 1.0-1.5, the ecological environment is the most superior. Most of the sandy lands are fixed or semi-fixed dunes, ranging from 2-20 m high, and dotted with small area drifting sand. There is stable humid sand layer in 5 mm below the surface of drifting sand.

Plants grow well in Horqin Sandy Land and Songnen Sandy Land. Besides herbs and shrubs, there are also arbor trees growths. As the top plant community developed in sandy lands of Songliao Plain, the elm forest presents a landscape including forest and grassland, and plays an important role in maintaining regional ecological balance as well as the eco-environment quality of Northeast China.

In this area, due to the favorable conditions of precipitation, the Xiliao River and its tributaries flow through the Horqin Sandy Land, as well as the Nenjiang River and its tributaries flow through the Songnen Sandy Land, and a lot of wetlands, small lakes are formed here. There are many water birds habitat, and other rare birds such as white cranes, red-crowned cranes, white-naped cranes, demoiselle cranes will stop here for foraging and supplementing physical strength during spring and autumn migration. Therefore, this place became a key area of the world famous East Asia-Australasia waterfowl migration route. There are Toad-headed lizards, sandgrouses, black grouses and other animals living and reproducing in sandy land.

Compared with other sandy land, this area has the best conditions of water and heat, and trees, shrubs and grass can all grow well here. As long as we take some measures, such as converting farmland to forests and pasture, closing sandy land for growing grass and so on, after 4-5 years of efforts, the dune vegetation coverage will be greatly increased, the drifting sand will gradually fixed, and the development trend of desertification will be effectively suppressed. Therefore, reducing or eliminating opening up pastures for farming or mining, protecting and improving grasslands, grazing reasonably and restricting grazing, and increasing vegetation and fixing sand are the main tasks of reasonably utilizing resources and protecting natural environment, which plays an important role in maintaining regional ecological balance and the quality of ecological environment, and it is also the key to recover and stabilize the ecological system of this area.

沙地榆树·内蒙古科尔沁沙地
榆树林是松辽平原沙地上发育的顶级植物群落，在这里构成了森林草原沙地景观，具有独特的群落种类构成和生态过程，对于维持区域生态平衡乃至东北地区生态环境质量均具有重要作用。

Sandy Elm Trees—Horqin Sandy Land, Inner Mongolia
As the top plant community developed in sandy lands of Songliao Plain, the elm forest presents a landscape including forest, grassland and sandy land, and possesses unique species composition of community and ecological processes, which plays an important role in maintaining regional ecological balance as well as the eco-environment quality of Northeast China.

沙水相连·内蒙古赤峰
沙丘和丘间湿地有时总是形影不离，相伴相生。

Sand and Water Are Connected to Each Other—Chifeng, Inner Mongolia
Dunes and wetlands which lied between dunes are always inseparable and accompanying with each other.

松嫩沙地鸟瞰·黑龙江齐齐哈尔

该沙地由松花江及其支流嫩江的沙质沉积物经风力吹扬而成。沙质底上分布着草场和农地，呈现出黄、绿相间的景观。

An Aerial View of Songnen Sandy Land—Qiqihar, Heilongjiang

The sandy land is made up of the accumulation of eolian sand deposits of Songhua River and its tributary Nenjiang River. Above the sandy base, grasslands and farmlands are distributed, presenting a yellow and green landscape.

科尔沁沙地冬日鸟瞰·内蒙古通辽

该沙地主要由西辽河沙质沉积物风力吹扬堆积而成，这里降水最为充沛，低洼处常常形成大量的浅水湿地，冬季结冰后呈现出一片特别的景观。

An Aerial View of the Winter Landscape in Horqin Sandy Lands—Tongliao, Inner Mongolia

The sandy land is mainly formed by the accumulation of eolian sand deposits in West Liaohe River. The precipitation here is the most abundant, and a large number of shallow water wetlands are often formed in low-lying areas. In winter, the frozen landscape brings people special enjoyment.

盐碱湖·内蒙古翁牛特旗
沙地低洼处常常积水成湖，水分蒸发后形成半咸湖、咸湖，盐碱泛起，白花花一片，这是该区常见的景观。

Saline Soda Lake—Ongniud Bannar, Inner Mongolia
In those low-lying areas of sandy lands, stagnant water often becomes a lake, and after evaporation of water, it forms brackish water lake or saline lake. Some salt blocks precipitated from the lake make everywhere in white and become a common landscape in this area.

湖畔盐产品·内蒙古翁牛特旗
盐湖析出的盐块堆积在一起,晾干后将运出作为工业原料利用。

Lakeside Salt Products—Ongniud Bannar, Inner Mongolia
The blocks of salt, precipitated from salt lake, pile up together, and after drying, them will be shipped out and used as an industrial raw material.

风向与沙向 · 内蒙古兴安盟
这个地区往往风势强劲，并且风旱同季。风向固定，沙向就固定，风与沙的关系在这里演绎得如此合拍，如此淋漓尽致。

Wind Direction and Sand Direction—Xing'an League, Inner Mongolia
There are often strong winds in this area and the wind season coincides with the dry season here. If the wind direction is fixed, the sand direction will be fixed. The relationship between the wind and the sand here is so well coordinated, so incisively and vividly.

沙丘植物·吉林白城

沙丘顶部，黄柳和沙米（近处矮株）生长良好。黄柳为内蒙古东与辽西沙丘上较普遍的灌木，是极佳的固沙树种，幼嫩枝叶为山羊和骆驼所喜食，秋天干枯后，山羊、绵羊、牛均喜食。

Dune Plants—Baicheng, Jilin

At the top of the dune, *Salix gordejevii* and shamie (the dwarf plant in front of the picture) grow well. *Salix gordejevii* is a more common shrub in Inner Mongolia and West Liaoning dunes. It is an excellent sand-fixing tree species. Its young foliage is a favorite for goats and camels. After its leaves turning dry in autumn, goats, sheep and cattle all like eating them.

林、草、沙、湿地一体·内蒙古巴林右旗

这里光、热、水条件最好,乔、灌、草都能生长,呈现出沙地、湿地、林地、草地相互交织、相互依存、共聚蓝天下的特殊生态系统。

Perfect Blending of Forest, Grass, Sand and Wetland— Bairin Right Banner, Inner Mongolia
The conditions of light, heat and water are the best here, and trees, shrubs and grass can all grow well here. As a result, it presents a special ecosystem in which sandy lands, wetlands, woodlands and grasslands, interwoven with each other, are interdependent and sharing the common blue sky.

1

2

3

4

1. 沙地榆树疏林生态系统·黑龙江松嫩沙地
The Sparse Elm Forest Ecosystem in Sandy Land— Songnen Sandy Land, Heilongjiang

2. 盐渍草地·内蒙古奈曼旗
The Saline Grassland—Naiman Banner, Inner Mongolia

3. 碱蓬草地·内蒙古库伦旗
The Alkali Grassland—Kulun Banner, Inner Mongolia

4. 沙芥—高大草本植物·内蒙古科尔沁沙地
The *Pugionium cornutum*, a Tall Herb— Horqin Sandy Land, Inner Mongolia

晚归丹顶鹤·黑龙江松嫩沙地

傍晚时节，丹顶鹤夫妻双双归来。松嫩沙地中的水泡子，是世界著名东亚—澳大利西亚水鸟迁徙路线上的关键地区，很多鹤类在春、秋两季迁徙途径，在这里停歇觅食、补充体力。

Homeward Red Crowned Crane Flock at Dusk — Songnen Sandy Land, Heilongjiang

These small lakes in Songnen Sandy Land are the key area of the world famous East Asia-Australasia waterfowl migration route, and many cranes migrate in spring and autumn, stopping here to hunt for food and to supplement their physical strength. The picture shows the red crowned crane couple returning in the evening.

（右页）朝飞白枕鹤·内蒙古科尔沁沙地

新的一天开始了，在沙丘间湿地，白枕鹤的雄鸟舒展翅膀，朝着清晨的阳光飞去。这里不仅是白枕鹤的迁徙路径地，也是它们的繁殖地。

(Opposite Page) A White-Naped Crane Flying in the Morning Light — Horqin Sandy Land, Inner Mongolia

A new day has begun, in the wetland between the sand dunes, a male white-naped crane is stretching his wings, and flying toward the early morning sun. Here is not only a migratory path to the white-naped cranes, but also their breeding ground.

1

2

3

4

1. 黄鼠
   A Hamste

2. 蜣螂
   A Desert Beetle

3. 沙蜥
   A Toad-headed Lizard

4. 草原雕
   Aquila nipalensis

典型的荒漠草原鸟——大鸨·吉林镇赉

大鸨主要栖息于开阔的平原、干旱草原、稀树草原和半荒漠地区，特别是在冬季和迁徙季节，也出现于邻近湿地的草地、农地。大鸨性耐寒、善奔走、不鸣叫、集群、机警，很难靠近。普通亚种繁殖于吉林、辽宁西部以及内蒙古等地。

The Great Bustard, a Typical Desert Steppe Bird — Zhenlai, Jilin

The great bustards mainly inhabit the open plains, arid grasslands, savannas and semi-desert areas; they also appear in grasslands and farmlands in adjacent to wetlands, especially in the winter and migratory seasons. The great bustards are cold-resistant and good at running. They barely tweet and are gregarious and alert. It is very hard to get close to them. The common subspecies breed in Jilin, Western Liaoning, and Inner Mongolia.

草原羊群·内蒙古科尔沁沙地
相比较其他区，本区水、热条件最佳，乔、灌、草都能生长，尊重自然规律，合理放牧，保护和改良草场，对于维持该区域生态平衡和可持续发展均具有极为重要的作用。

Flocks of Sheep on the Steppe— Horqin Sandy Land, Inner Mongolia
Compared with other areas, the water and heat conditions in this area are the best, and trees, shrubs and grass can grow here. As long as people respect the laws of nature, make reasonable grazing, and protect and improve grasslands, it will play a very important role in maintaining regional ecological balance and sustainable development.

找回羔羊·黑龙江松嫩沙地
人们可以找回羔羊、找回羊群，人们更应该找回优良草原、找回生态系统的平衡、找回人与自然和谐的良好环境。

Retrieving the Lost Lamb — Songnen Sandy Land, Heilongjiang
People can retrieve the lamb and find flocks of sheep; people should also retrieve the grassland, recover the balance of the ecological system, and find a good environment for the harmony between man and nature.

2 内蒙古高原
半干旱干旱区
The Semi-arid and Arid Areas in the Inner Mongolia Plateau

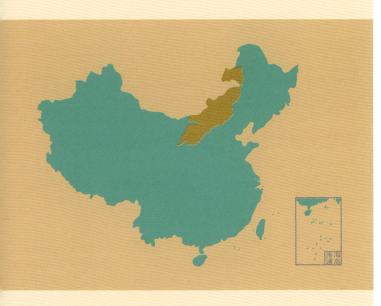

（前页）离北京最近的沙漠·内蒙古库布齐沙漠
中国第七大沙漠，西、北、东三面均以黄河为界，沙源主要来自古代黄河冲积物和阴山西段狼山地区山前洪积物，形态以沙丘链和格状沙丘为主。
(Previous Page) The Desert Closest to Beijing — Kubuqi Desert, Inner Mongolia
The seventh largest in China, Kubuqi Desert was bounded by the Yellow River in the west, the north and the east. The main source came from the ancient Yellow River alluvial material and also the Langshan district diluvium, which is located in western segment of the Yinshan Mountains. It mainly takes the form of dune chain and trellis dune.

（从左至右）
乌珠穆沁沙地·内蒙古西乌珠穆沁旗
草原上的流动沙丘·内蒙古巴彦淖尔
沙地樟子松·内蒙古红花尔基
毛腿沙鸡·内蒙古苏尼特右旗
草原蒙古包·内蒙古乌兰浩特
(From Left to Right)
Uzhumuqin Sandy Land — West Uzhumuqin Banner, Inner Mongolia
The Flowing Sand Dunes on the Grassland — Bayan Nur, Inner Mongolia
Pinus sylvestris var. Mongolica — Honghua Erji, Inner Mongolia
Syrrhaptes paradoxus — Sonid Right Banner, Inner Mongolia
The Steppe Mongolian Yurts — Ulanhot, Inner Mongolia

内蒙古高原半干旱干旱区

该区域处于中国地势第二级阶梯的东北，范围东至大兴安岭西麓，南至黄土高原（大致以长城为界），西至贺兰山一线，北至中蒙边界，属于温带季风气候，海拔 800～1500m，局部可降至 600m，自东南向西北愈趋干旱，降水量自东南缘的 450～520mm 依次下降到西北缘的 150mm 以下，干燥度由 4.0 增至 16.0。该区域气候干燥，日照充足，区域内无较大河流，且多为内流间歇河。沙地、沙漠、戈壁依次从东南向西北略呈弧形分布。东部为温带半干旱气候，发育了半干旱沙地景观，为呼伦贝尔沙地、乌珠穆沁沙地等。西部为温带干旱气候，发育了干旱沙漠、戈壁景观，为巴音戈壁、库布齐沙漠、浑善达克沙地、毛乌素沙地等。西部沙地与东北部沙地相比，流沙分布面积显著增加，呈现出流沙与固定半固定沙丘相互交错的景观。毛乌素沙地地处鄂尔多斯腹地，这一地区大多为固定半固定沙丘。

内蒙古高原是我国最大的天然牧场，植物种类以多年旱生中温带草本植物占优势，且有旱生小灌木和小半灌木成分。在浑善达克沙地东北缘生长着独特、珍贵的树种——沙地云杉，形成目前世界上同类地区仅存的一片沙地云杉林。大兴安岭及海拉尔以西、以南沙地及石砾沙土地区有沙地樟子松。由东向西，随着降水量的逐渐减少，牧草的生长状况也越来越差。植物资源主要有甘草、麻黄、枸杞、银柴胡、沙棘、沙芥等。

浑善达克沙地是中国著名的有水沙地之一，在沙地中分布着众多的小湖、水泡子和沙泉，大批候鸟从南方飞回，来到查干诺尔湖及附近栖息，有国家重点保护的丹顶鹤、白枕鹤、灰鹤、蓑羽鹤等珍稀鸟类。毛乌素沙地有国家一级重点保护野生动物——遗鸥，为世界上濒临灭绝动物之一，也是世界最大的繁殖种群。荒漠草原还有狐狸、狼、草原雕、雪鸮、黄爪隼、毛腿沙鸡、石鸡等，靠近林子还有狍子、乌林鸮、长尾林鸮等。

此区属半干旱区向干旱区的过渡区域，除了气候变化原因外，人类的活动干扰是该区荒漠生态系统破坏、土地退化和荒漠化的根本原因。因此，改变人类不合理的生产生活方式，合理利用草场，退耕限牧，封山封滩封沙、还林还草还湿是保护这里的生态环境，保证人与自然和谐、社会可持续发展的根本。

Arid and Semi-arid Areas in the Inner Mongolia Plateau

It stretches from the Greater Hinggan's west piedmont in the east to the line of Helan Mountain in the west, and the north connects Sino-Mongolian border and south reach to the Loess Plateau (roughly divided by the Great Wall), belonging to temperate monsoon climate zone. The elevation is from 800 m to 1500 m, with a localized drop to 600 m. The precipitation drops from 450-520 mm in the southeast to below 150 mm in the northwest, with the aridity increasing from 4.0 to 16.0. The area is dry with abundant sunshine. There are no large rivers and most of the rivers are intermittent. From southeast to northwest, the sand, desert and Gobi are distributed in the shape of arc. The eastern area is the temperate and semi-arid climate, developing a semi-arid sandy landscape, such as the Hulunbuir Sandy Land and Uzhumuqin Sandy Land. The western area is the temperate arid climate, developing the arid desert and Gobi landscape, such as Bayin Gobi, Kubuqi Desert, Hunshandake Sandy Land and Maowusu Sandy Land. Compared with the northeast sandy land, the sandy land in the west has much more drifting sand. Thus, it appears a landscape that the drifting sand is intertwined with the fix and semi-fix dune. Maowusu Sandy Land is located in the hinterland of Ordos, most of this area is fix and semi-fix dune.

Inner Mongolia Plateau is the largest natural pasture in China, the plants are dominated by the perennial xerophyte mesothermal herbs, mixed with small xerophyte shrubs and semi-shrubs. *Picea mongolica* is a unique and precious tree in the northeastern margin of Hunshandake Sandy Land, forming the only sandy spruce forest in the same kinds of places in the world. The *Pinus sylvestris* var. *mongolica* is founded in the west of Greater Khingan mountains and Hailaer. From east to west, with the gradual reduction of precipitation, the growth condition of grass is getting worse. Plant resources are mainly *Glycyrrhiza uralensis*, ephedra, wolfberry, starwort root, *Hippophae rhamnoides*, *Pugionium cornutum* and so on.

Hunshandake is one of the famous sandy lands with waters in China. Numerous small lakes, ponds and springs are distributed in the sandy land. There is a large number of migratory birds flying from the south perched in Chagan Noel Lake and nearby, including national key protected birds red-crowned crane, white-naped crane, grey crane, demoiselle crane and several other rare birds. Maowusu Sandy Land is home to a Category One National Protected Animal and the world's endangered species–relic gull (*Ichthyaetus relictus*), with the world's largest breeding population. In desert grassland, there are also fox, wolf, steppe eagle (*Aquila nipalensis*), snow owl (*Bubo scandiacus*), lesser kestrel (*Falco naumanni*), Pallas's sandgrouse (*Syrrhaptes paradoxus*), chukar partridge (*Alectoris chukar*) and so on. Near the woods, there are also roe deer, great grey owl (*Strix nebulosi*), and ural owl (*Strix uralensis*) and so on.

This region is a transition zone between arid and semi-arid areas. In addition to the causes of climate change, disturbance of human activities is the root cause of desert ecosystem destruction, land degradation and desertification in this region. In order to maintain the environment protection, the harmony between human and the nature and the sustainable development of society, the prime way is changing people's unreasonable production methods and life style, which includes putting grassland into rational use, restricting grazing, converting farmlands to forests, grasslands and wetlands, as well as enclosing mountains, sheets and dunes.

内蒙古荒漠的典型代表·内蒙古苏尼特左旗
苏尼特左旗的巴润查干淖尔是一个封闭的湖泊，该湖是高大沙丘的共生物，而高大沙丘是由固定、半固定和流动沙丘三种沙丘类型共同组成，体现了处于季风边缘区干旱半干旱过渡带荒漠的综合特征。

A Typical Representative of Inner Mongolia Desert — Sonid Left Banner, Inner Mongolia
Barun Chagan Nur of Sonid Left Banner is a closed lake. This lake is the symbiosis of lofty sand dune, which is composed of fixed, semi-fixed and shifting dunes. It reflects the comprehensive characteristics of the arid and semi-arid desert transitional zone in the monsoon region.

沙坡头·宁夏中卫

这里是本区的最西端，沙坡头南靠重峦叠嶂的祁连山余脉——香山，北连沙峰林立的腾格里沙漠，中间被奔腾而下的黄河横穿而过。在沙与河之间，是一片郁郁葱葱的绿洲。这里集广漠、大河、高山、绿洲为一体，具西北风光之雄奇，兼江南景色之秀美。

Shapotou —Zhongwei, Ningxia

As the westernmost part in this area, it is bordered in the south by ranges of Qilian mountains—Xiangshan Mountain, shared boundary with the northern serried Tengger Desert, traversed by the Yellow River in the middle. Between the sand and the river, there is a lush oasis. It integrates vast desert, big rivers, high mountains and oasis, creating a landscape featuring both the magnificent northwest scenery and the beautiful scenery of the south.

离北京最近的沙地·内蒙古浑善达克沙地

浑善达克沙地受东亚季风及其变迁的影响,其环境在温带荒漠草原和森林草原之间波动变化,出现一系列沙漠扩展与沙丘固定、沙漠收缩与沙丘活化的推拉波动现象,"推之则荒、拉之则绿"。在沙丘间发育着榆林疏林、灌丛和草甸,多为固定或半固定沙丘,丘间多甸子地。

The Sand Source Closest to Beijing — Hunshandake Sandy Land

Under the influence of the East Asian monsoon and its changes, its environment fluctuates between temperate desert steppe and forest steppe. This leads to a series fluctuations between desert extension and dune fixation, between desert contraction and dune reactivation. "Making desert or oasis depends on our choice." Sparse elm forest, shrub and meadow developed among the dunes, most of which are fixed or semi-fixed, and marshy grassland that is composed of light yellow sand are interspersed among hills.

1. 寄生在梭梭树下的植物——肉苁蓉
   Plants that Parasitizes under Sacsaoul Trees—*Cistanche deserticola*

2. 盐渍土指示植物——白刺
   Dominant Plant of Saline Soil—*Nitraria tangutorum*

3. 多年生半灌木——花棒
   A Perennial Shrub—*Hedysarum scoparium*

沙地云杉·内蒙古白音敖包
这里是目前世界上同类地区仅存的一片沙地云杉林。在这干旱而又贫瘠的生长环境中，沙地云杉能够长到25～30 m高，胸径22～36 cm，非常难得。其盘根错节的树根犹如游龙一般，十分有利于聚拢散碎的细沙，能够有效地控制沙漠的流动。

Picea mongolica—Bayan Oboo, Inner Mongolia
Now it is the only *Picea mongolica* in the similar area in the world. In such a growing environment, dry and almost barren, it is rare to see that the trees grow up to 25–30 m with diameters at breast height between 22 cm and 36 cm. Its gnarled roots twisted in and out of the earth like a slow brown serpents, which is helpful in gathering scattered pieces of sand and controlling the flow of the desert effectively.

踽踽狼行·河北围场
狼是以肉食为主的杂食性动物，是生物链中极为关键的一环。中国长期以来把狼作为害兽加以消灭，加上其栖息地不断缩小，近几十年中狼的数量越来越少，许多过去狼的分布区已不见其踪迹。

Lonely Wolf — Weichang, Heibei
Wolf is the meat-based omnivorous animals, and an extremely key component in the food chain. Wolves have been hunted for long as pests in China. With the shrinking of the habitats, the population of the wolf is getting fewer and fewer in recent decades, disappearing from many areas where the wolf used to distribute.

惬意·内蒙古锡林郭勒盟
赤狐主要生活在森林、草原、沙地及丘陵地带，居住于树洞或土穴中，夜行性动物，主要以兔及鼠类为食，也吃野禽、蛙、昆虫等，是草原、荒漠草原生态系统的顶级肉食性动物。

Cosy Life — Xilingol League, Inner Mongolia
Distributed in forests, grasslands, deserts and hills, the red fox is nocturnal animals, which lives in tree holes or soil caves. It is the top predators in the grassland ecosystem on a diet of hares and rodents, as well as wildfowl, frogs, insects and so on.

雪鸮与草垛 · 内蒙古新巴尔虎右旗

雪鸮繁殖于环北极冻土带以及北极圈内，是迁徙的鸟类，在我国少见。中国呼伦贝尔是其分布的南缘。与很多鸮类不同的是，雪鸮白天活动晚上休息，偶尔也在黄昏后捕猎，猎捕野兔、鼠类、游禽、涉禽等。

Snow Owl (*Bubo scandiacus*) and Hayrick — New Barag Right Banner, Inner Mongolia

Snow owl is migratory birds, breeding inside the arctic and the arctic tundra. It is rare in China of which Hulunbuir is the south edge for its distribution. Unlike other strigiformes, snow owl is diurnal-active during the day and resting during the night, hunting hares, rodents, natatores, waders and so on in daytime and occasionally after dusk.

荒漠地区的雉 · 内蒙古大青山

石鸡为中型雉类，栖息于低山丘陵地带的岩石坡和沙石坡上以及草原、荒漠等地区，喜集群，以草本植物和灌木的嫩芽、叶、种子和昆虫等为食，是少数能在荒漠地区栖息的雉类之一。

Phasianidae in Desert Area — Daqing Mountain, Inner Mongolia

Alectoris chukar is a medium-sized phasianidae, which inhabits rocky slope and sandy slope in hilly land or grassland and desert areas. It feeds on the buds of herbaceous plants and bush, seeds, insects and so on, and it tends to flock together. *Alectoris chukar* is one of the few pheasants that can inhabit in desert areas.

回眸·内蒙古杭锦旗

黄爪隼栖息于旷野、荒漠草地、河谷疏林等，以鼠类、小型鸟类、甲虫等昆虫为食。和荒漠地区的很多猛禽食性一样，黄爪隼飞翔技术高超，捕猎技术一流，对于控制草原、荒漠草原鼠害起着极其关键的作用。

Lingering Eye Sights — Hanggin Banner, Inner Mongolia

Falco naumanni inhabits open fields, deserts, grasslands, river valleys, and open forests. It feeds on rodents, small birds, beetles and other insects. Like any other raptors' diets in desert areas, it is a super-skilled flyer and hunter that plays a key role in preventing grassland and desert steppe from rodent damage.

母爱·陕西神木

遗鸥几乎是最后才被发现的新鸥种，因此得名。遗鸥栖息并且繁殖于毛乌素沙地的淡水或咸水湖中，越冬于渤海湾，是地球上极少数东西向迁徙的鸟类。

Mother's Love —Shenmu, Shaanxi

Larus relictus is named because it is almost the latest discovery. It inhabits and breeds in freshwater or salt lakes in the Maowusu Sandy Land, and winters in the Bohai Gulf. *Larus relictus* is among a tiny handful of birds that migrate between east and west.

求偶·内蒙古呼伦贝尔

黑琴鸡发情争斗时有相对固定的场地，俗称"斗鸡盘"，雄鸟几只或十几只飞来后开始鸣叫，尾羽垂直向上展开呈扇状，翅膀下垂，不时地跳起来与其他雄鸟搏斗，胜利者可得到雌鸟的青睐，享有交配权。

Courtship — Hulunbuir, Inner Mongolia

Black grouse has a relatively fixed place in estrus, it is commonly known as "the roster battlefield". A few or more roosters wheel and chirpon the field, and occasionally provoke others with the fan-shaped tail pointing skywards while the wings hanging down. The one who prevails in the competition will win the favor of the female bird and entitled to mating.

林场新住户·内蒙古牙克石

随着野生动物保护、防沙治沙、天然林保护等工程的实施,很多森工企业转产搬迁,由砍树人变成护林人。拆除与废弃的林场住房迎来了新住户——长尾林鸮。长尾林鸮主要以鼠类等为食。

New Residents in Forest Farm — Yakeshi, Inner Mongolia

With the implementation of such programs as wildlife protection, desertification prevention and control, and natural forest protection, many forest industry enterprises have become protectors instead of destroyer. Through adjusting industry structures and relocating houses, the abandoned forest farm ushered in a new resident—*Strix uralensis*, which mainly feed on rodents.

大草原的羊群·内蒙古锡林郭勒草原

本区有五大草原，自东向西顺次是：呼伦贝尔草原、科尔沁草原、锡林郭勒草原、乌兰察布草原以及鄂尔多斯半荒漠草原，占到全区域面积的 80% 以上，是蒙古民族的主要生活分布地，也是国家最重要的畜牧业基地。草原生态系统崩溃或者退化，极易成为沙地。

Flocks of Sheep in Grassland — Xilingol Steppe, Inner Mongolia

There are five grasslands in this area, from east to west: Hulunbuir Grassland, Horqin Steppe, Xilingol Steppe, Ulanqab Steppe and Ordos Semi-desert Grassland, which account for more than 80% of the whole area. It is the main populated area for Mongolian nationality, and also the most important basis for animal husbandry in the country. Once the grassland ecosystem collapses or degrades, it can become the sandy land easily.

长城边，古道旁，芳草萋萋凉·宁夏盐池
中国古代长城多是为了抵御北方游牧民族入侵而修建的。在中国中西部，长城基本为农区与牧区的分界线，也大致是荒漠区的南界。

On the Ancient Road by the Great Wall, Desolated Grass Interspersed — Yanchi, Ningxia

In ancient China, the Great Wall was built to resist the invasion from the northern nomadic people. In China's central and western regions, the mid-west of China, the Great Wall is basically the demarcation line between agricultural and pastoral areas, as well as the southern boundary of the desert area.

沙进人退·陕西毛乌素沙地

原来的人类定居点、盐场被沙漠包围,被流动沙丘逐步覆盖,呈现出的是沙进人退不可逆转的局面。

When the Sand Advances, the People Retreats — Maowusu Sandy Land

The previous settlements and saltern are surrounded by the desert and covered by the shifting dunes, presenting an irreversible situation that when the sand encroaches, the people retreat.

沙漠太阳能发电场·宁夏中卫

利用沙漠地区光、热充足的优势,建设大面积的太阳能发电场,一可以发挥再生能源低成本、无污染的优势,二还能够利用太阳能板的庇荫效果增加植被覆盖,是人们利用沙漠、发展沙产业的一种好办法。

Solar Power Station in Desert — Zhongwei, Ningxia

Taking advantages of light and heat in desert area, the construction of solar energy power field in large area is a wise chose. The renewable energy is produced with low cost and no pollution. In the meanwhile, the vegetation coverage is increased by the shade effect of solar panels, which is a good method for people to take advantage of desert and develop industry.

人进沙退的典型·宁夏沙坡头

沙坡头位于腾格里沙漠东南缘，黄河西岸边。每当狂风肆虐时，这里便飞沙走石，连绵起伏的流动沙丘掩埋村庄，吞噬良田。为了阻止沙漠对包兰铁路、公路的严重威胁，这里试验成功了中国人的治沙"魔方"——草方格。沙坡头治沙防护体系保证了包兰铁路畅通无阻50多年，为国家直接或间接创造经济效益数百亿元，被联合国环境规划署授予"全球环境保护500佳单位"的称号。

When the People Advances, the Sand Retreats — Shapotou, Ningxia

Shapotou is located in the southeastern edge of the Tengger Desert, the west bank of the Yellow River. Whenever the strong wind blows, with flying and rolling pebbles, the sand dunes will swallow villages and farmlands. In order to prevent the Baolan Railway and Expressway from serious threat of desert, the straw checkerboard, which is the Chinese people's "cube", has been successfully applied. The desert control system in Shapotou has ensured the Baolan Railway to be unimpeded for fifty years, and also directly or indirectly produced billions of economic benefit. It was awarded "Global 500 Roll of Honor" by the United Nations Environment Program.

治沙"魔方"——草方格·宁夏沙坡头

草方格沙障是用麦草、稻草、芦苇等材料，在流动沙丘上扎设成方格状的挡风墙。其机理一是能使地面粗糙，减小风力，阻挡沙粒滚动；二是可以截留水分，提高沙层含水量，最终有利于表面结皮的形成和固沙植物的存活，起到固沙和培育植被的奇效。

Desert Controlling Cube, the Straw Checkerboard — Shapotou, Ningxia

Straw checkerboard barrier is a wind-break wall in square shape in the shifting dunes, which is made of wheat straw, rice straw, reed and other materials. It can roughen the ground and reduce the wind, besides, it can also intercept water and improve the moisture content of the sand. Ultimately, it can conducive to the formation of surface crust and the survival of sand plants, so as to fix sand and cultivate vegetation effectively.

3

阿拉善高原与河西走廊干旱极干旱区

The Arid and Extremely Arid Areas in the Alxa Plateau and the Hexi Corridor

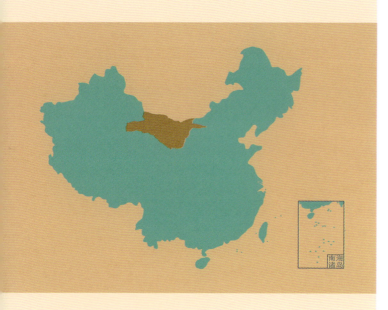

阿拉善高原与河西走廊干旱极干旱区

该区域为中国地势第二级阶梯的正北部分，范围北至中国与蒙古国边界，东为贺兰山，南以祁连山—阿尔金山与青海省为界，西至马鬃山戈壁，这里属大陆性干旱气候。由于地处大陆腹地，湿润的海洋季风鞭长莫及，自东而西年降水量渐少，干燥度渐大。年降水量从东部贺兰山的200mm左右向西递减到黑河下游的50mm左右，敦煌的36.8mm，干燥度则从4.0左右递增到24.0左右。气候干燥，冷热变化剧烈，风大沙多，昼夜温差平均达15℃左右。

该区域流沙、戈壁广布，大部分海拔1300m左右，地势由南向北缓倾，地面起伏不大，仅少数山地超过2000m，最低处居延海附近为820m。该区荒漠的主要特点是以流动沙丘和戈壁为主，主要分布有巴丹吉林、腾格里、乌兰布和三大沙漠。岩漠主要分布在如马鬃山、雅布赖山、贺兰山等的山前地带，砾漠则主要分布在其外围地带或沙漠周边。

该区域的黄河、石羊河、黑河、疏勒河等较大河流均源自青藏高原，沙漠区内有许多湖泊和时令湖。地表水除东缘的黄河为过境水外，其余均为内流河。

该区除高山生长有原始森林、古河畔有胡杨林、荒漠草原有梭梭林外，广大地区以极其稀疏的灌木、半灌木为主，甚至大片区域几无寸草。地带性植被主要由超旱生灌木、半灌木和超旱生半乔木组成。东部植被具有明显的草原化特征，形成较独特的草原化荒漠类型。西部砾质戈壁分布有典型的荒漠植被，如红砂、膜果麻黄、裸果木等群落类型，流动沙丘上常见有沙拐枣、沙米、沙芥等，固定沙丘上常见有柽柳、白刺等。河流冲积平原上分布有芦苇、芨芨草、甘草、骆驼刺等组成的盐生草甸。

区域内有不少珍稀野生动物，包括国家重点保护野生动物野骆驼、蒙古野驴、鹅喉羚、盘羊、北山羊等，在腾格里沙漠中间的天然湿地偶有野鸭、天鹅等水禽在这里停歇补充体力。高鼻羚羊、普氏野马等荒漠珍稀原生动物，通过人工重引入生长良好。

该区域的石羊河过去曾注入淡水湖白亭海，白亭海现已完全干涸。黑河曾经断流，下游的居延海也一度干涸，部分地区生态问题相当严重，尤其额济纳地区是中国沙尘暴的主要策源地。在该地区，需要对仅存的乔木、灌木、草本植被采取最严格的保护措施，使其不再受任何破坏。对于江河源头的森林要严格保护，几大河流流域要限量用水、合理分配用水，对于荒漠草原区必须进行全面退牧还草的生态恢复工程，采取禁牧封育、飞播封育等工程措施，才能有效恢复和保护好这里异常脆弱的生态环境。

（前页）荒漠大成·甘肃阿克塞

石山、岩漠、砾漠、沙漠、河流、乔木、灌木、沙地、湿地、盐碱地、草地，中国荒漠的所有元素几乎都集中在这个视野里；黑、灰、橙、黄、棕、白、绿、蓝，中国荒漠的所有颜色也几乎都集中在这个画面里，可谓中国荒漠集大成者也！

(Previous Page) Aggregation in Desert—Akesai, Gansu

Rocky hill, hamada, gravel desert, sand desert, river, tree, shrub, sandy land, wetland, salt marsh, grassland, all the elements of desert in China are concentrated in this perspective; black, gray, orange, yellow, brown, white, green, blue, all the colors of the Chinese desert are also concentrated in this picture. What a synthesis of China's desert!

（从左至右）
戈壁与公路·甘肃敦煌
阿尔金山与库姆塔格沙漠·甘肃阿克塞
旱生植物—骆驼刺·内蒙古腾格里沙漠
沙漠之舟—骆驼·甘肃酒泉
月牙泉—甘肃敦煌
(From Left to Right)
Gobi and Expressway—Dunhuang, Gansu
Altun Mountains and Kumtag Desert—Akesai, Gansu
Alhagi sparsifolia, Xerphyte —Tengger Desert, Inner Mongolia
Camel, "Ships of the Desert" —Jiuquan, Gansu
Crescent Spring —Dunhuang, Gansu

The Arid and Extremely Arid Areas in the Alxa Plateau and the Hexi Corridor

Reaching Sino-Mongolia border on the north, Helan Mountain on the east, the border of Qilian Mountain, Aerjin Mountain and Qinghai Province on the south, Gobi of Mazong Mountain on the west, this area belongs to continental arid climate. As located in the hinterland of the mainland, the wet oceanic wind hardly gets here. From east to west, the precipitation gradually decreased, from around 200 mm in Helan Mountain to 50 mm in the lower reaches of Heihe River, and 36.8 mm in Dunhuang, while the drought index increases from 4.0 to 24.0 or so. The climate is dry and dramatic with vast sand and strong wind, and the diurnal temperature variation is about 15 °C.

In this area, the drifting sand and Gobi are widely distributed; most of the elevation is about 1300 m; the terrain is gently dipping from south to north, and the ground has little undulation; only a few mountains exceed 2000 m, and at the lowest point near Juyan Lake, the land rises merely 820 m above sea level. The key features of this desert are mainly shifting dunes and Gobi deserts, where Badan Jaran Desert, Tengger Desert and Ulan Buh Desert are distributed. Hamada is mainly spread over the piedmont areas such as Mazong Mountain, Yabrai Mountain and Helan Mountain. While gravel desert is mainly distributed in its periphery zones or surrounding desert.

The major rivers, such as the Yellow River, Shiyang River, Heihe River and Shule River, are all originated from the Tibetan Plateau, and there are many lakes and seasonal lakes in this region. Except the Yellow River at the east edge, which is the transit water, the rest surface waters are interior rivers.

Except the original forests grow in high hills, *Populus euphratica* forests grow in the ancient river, *Haloxylon* forests grow in the desert grassland, the rest places are mainly covered with extremely sparse bushes and semi-bushes, or even worse, with nothing. Zonal vegetation is mainly composed of super xerophytic shrubs, subshrub and super xerophytic arbor. The eastern vegetation has obvious grassland characteristics and formed a unique type of grassland desert. The western gravel desert has typical desert vegetation, such as *Reaumuria songarica*, *Ephedra przewalskii*, *Gymnocarpos przewalskii* and other community types. *Calligonum mongolicum*, *Agriophyllum squarrosum* and *Pugionium cornutum* are common on the shifting dunes; *Tamarix* and *Nitraia tangutorum* are common in the fixed dunes. The saline meadow, such as reeds, *Achnatherum splendens*, *Glycyrrhiza uralensis* and *Alhagi sparsifolia* are distributed in the alluvial plain.

There are many rare wild animals in the region, including such national key protected wild animals as *Camelus ferus*, *Equus hemionus*, *Gazella subgutturosa*, argali sheep and *Capra sibirica*. In the natural wetland in the Tengger desert, there are mallards, swans and other water birds stopping in this place to replenish their strength. The rare native animals in desert such as *Saiga tatarica* and *Equus ferus* ssp. *przewalskii* grow well through artificial reintroduction.

The Shiyang River used to empty into the freshwater lake Baitinghai, which has completely dried up. The Heihe River has been cut off, and the Juyan Lake in the lower reaches once also dried up. Its ecological problems are quite serious, especially Ejin area is the main source of sand and dust storms in China. In this region, the remaining trees, shrubs and vegetation are required to be protected from any damages with the most strict measures. We should strictly protect those forests located in the source of rivers and limit water use and distribute the water use of major rivers rationally in several large basins. This desert grassland must carry out the ecological restoration project, which include putting grassland into rational use, converting farmland and grazing land to grassland, aerial seeding and closing so as to effectively recover and protect the fragile ecological environment.

沙丘晨曦·内蒙古巴丹吉林沙漠

巴丹吉林沙漠是中国第三大沙漠，沙漠腹地的必鲁图沙峰海拔1609 m，相对高度逾500 m，有"沙海珠穆朗玛峰"之称，为世界第一高沙峰。该地气候极为干旱，年降水量不足40 mm，但是沙漠中的湖泊竟然多达100多个。近年来，由于气候干旱、大风及人为活动的影响，巴丹吉林沙漠面积不断增大，并以平均每年15～20 m的速度向腾格里沙漠靠拢，两大沙漠已成握手合拢之势。

Sand Dunes at Dawn — Badan Jaran Desert, Inner Mongolia

The Badan Jaran Desert is the third largest desert in China. The heartland of this desert is Bilutu Sand Peak at an elevation of 1609 m, the world's tallest one with a relative height of over 500 m, thus named "the Everest in Desert". This region is extremely arid, with less than 40 mm of annual precipitation, but there are more than 100 lakes. In recent years, because of dry climate, strong wind and human activities, the Badan Jaran Desert is expending at the speed of 15–20 m a year on average towards Tengger Desert. These two deserts tend to join up together.

一水之隔·甘肃敦煌

库姆塔格沙漠的东缘在本区域，十余条重要地表径流穿过沙漠向罗布泊洼地汇集。厚重的原岩石地貌与堆积的高大沙丘之间一水之隔，生动地记录了该干旱区气候、水系及地理环境演化的历史。

Across the River—Dunhuang, Gansu

The east edge of Kumtag Desert, where more than ten important surface runoffs are crossing and directing to the Lop Nor Depression, is in this region. The thick proto-rocky landscape and the piled high hills are separated by a strip of water, which vividly recorded the evolution history of the arid climate, water system and geographical environment.

石臼山·内蒙古阿拉善右旗

这里定向且强烈的风力常年作用在砂岩石上，裹挟着不断产生的沙粒，在岩石表面刻画着、吹蚀着、旋转着，形成了一个个凹坑、洞穴，甚至琢穿整个岩石，这里犹如一座天然宏伟的石雕艺术馆，鬼斧神工，使人倍感大自然的魔力。

Shijiu Mountain—Alxa Right Banner, Inner Mongolia

The directional and intense wind affects the sand stones all through the year. Depicting, blowing and spinning, the wind passes through the rocks with grains of sand. This region, pitted with cracks and holes, is like a natural magnificent stone carving museum. The nature's creations make people have a strong feeling about its magic.

沙漠天鹅湖·内蒙古阿拉善左旗

贺兰山背影下的腾格里沙漠,孕育了无数的湖泊,天鹅湖是其中之一。湖的一半是淡水湖,另一半则是咸水湖,包括大天鹅在内的很多鸟类在这里栖息。

Swan Lake in Desert — Alxa Left Banner, Inner Mongolia
Against the Helan Mountains, Tengger Desert has fostered countless lakes, among which is the Swan Lake. Many birds, including swans, inhabit this half freshwater and half saltwater lake.

老天爷·内蒙古腾格里沙漠

"腾格里"蒙古语意为"老天爷",腾格里沙漠寓意为茫茫流沙有如渺无边际的天空。沙漠南越长城,东抵贺兰山,西至雅布赖山,为中国第四大沙漠。

The God — Tengger Desert, Inner Mongolia
"Tengri" means "God" in Mongolian, and the Tengger Desert means the boundless drifting sand which is like the sky. The desert crossing the Great Wall in the south, reaching the Helan Mountain in the east, stretching Yabrai Hill in the west, and it is the China's fourth-largest desert.

祁连山体·甘肃张掖

狼山、贺兰山、祁连山和马鬃山形成一个巨大的"U"字形山体链。这个山体链将本区从东、南、西三个方向团团围住，起到了地理隔离作用，又因区域内常年强劲的西北风，使本区山体成为了风蚀作用的主要对象和沙石供给的重要源头。

The Qilian Mountain Range — Zhangye, Gansu

The mountain range encircled this area with Langshan Mountain, Ho-lan Mountain, Qilian Mountain and Mazong Mountain from the east, south and west respectively. This U-shaped mountain range plays the role of geographical isolation, and because of the strong wind from northwest in this region, the Mountain Range has become the main object of wind erosion and the important source of sand supply.

贺兰沧桑·宁夏石嘴山

贺兰山处于年 400 mm 降水量线上，是我国季风区与非季风区的界线，其西为大漠的腾格里沙漠，东为"天下黄河富宁夏"的银川平原，为该地域干旱与半干旱区的分界线。

Vicissitudes of Helan Mountain—Shizuishan, Ningxia

Helan Mountain, on the 400 mm precipitation line, is the boundary between monsoon and non-monsoon regions. There are Tengger Desert in the west and Yinchuan Plain, at the heart of Ningxia enriched by the Yellow River, in the east. It is also the demarcation line between the arid and semiarid region in this area.

沙水情缘·内蒙古阿拉善右旗

千里连绵起伏的沙丘如同凝固的波浪，一块块海子如小岛镶嵌在沙海之中，海子湛蓝、亲切、柔美，大漠浩瀚、雄浑、苍凉。线条和颜色展现出它们壮阔且迷人的风范。大漠和海子相依相偎，共同构成大自然的神奇篇章。

Between Sand and Water—Alxa Right Banner, Inner Mongolia

The endless undulating dunes are interspersed with pieces of lakes. The dunes like solidified waves and the lakes are islands on the desert sea. The blue, warm and soft lakes are perfect companies to the vast, powerful and desolate desert. The combination of lines and colors show its magnificent and charming demeanor. The picture of desert speckling with lakes constitute the magic chapter of nature.

沙海星空 · 内蒙古巴丹吉林沙漠
月亮就要升起来了，大沙丘前寂静的海子让星空留下了最后默默的念想。

The Desert Sea under the Night Sky — Badan Jaran Desert, Inner Mongolia
The moon is about to rise, the quiet lake before the large dunes left the sky with the final silent admiration.

沙的源泉·甘肃祁连山
在千万年自然力的作用下，高山岩石剥离并逐步扩展，形成了岩漠、砾漠、沙漠、盐漠。

The Sand Source—Qilian Mountain, Gansu
The mountain rocks peeled off and gradually expanded with the nature's power for millions of years, forming hamada, gravel desert, sand desert and salt desert.

沙的形态·内蒙古腾格里沙漠
在长时期各种风力的作用下，沙石颗粒移动并堆积，不断生出沙丘、沙垄、沙面、沙纹。
The Formation of Desert—Tengger Desert, Inner Mongolia
In a long time, the sand grains move and accumulate under the power of wind, continuously forming sand dunes, sand ridges, sand surface and sand ripples.

茫茫黑戈壁·甘肃马鬃山

中蒙边境马鬃山附近方圆二百多千米,其一马平川的黑砾石滩是著名的"黑戈壁"。黑戈壁就是黑色的砾漠,其有两个显著特征:一是砾石相当普遍,经受风沙磨蚀后表面十分光滑;二是砾石表面的水分蒸发时将所溶解的矿物残留,天长日久形成了乌黑发亮的表层。

The Boundless and Indistinct Black Gobi Desert—Mazong Mountain, Gansu
As the Sino-Mongolian border, Mazong Mountain has a circumference of 200 km. The boundless black grave plain is famous as "Black Gobi". It is a black gravel desert, which has two prominent characteristics: the first is that the gravel is quite common and the surface is very smooth after sand abrasion. The second is when the water on the gravel surface evaporates, the residual minerals formed the black surface over time.

石臼群与沙的形成·内蒙古阿拉善右旗

沙质岩石在千万年风的强力作用下,形成了石臼群,剥离下来的大小碎粒继续风化,历经沧桑,逐渐形成颗粒越来越小、各型各态的沙漠。

Formation of Stone Mortar Groups and Sand—Alxa Right Banner, Inner Mongolia
Under the strong action of wind for millions of years, the sandy rock was shaped to stone mortar groups. As the wind erosion goes on, the particles fell off from the rocks get tinier. Over a long period of time, deserts of different types are created.

荒野大戈壁·甘肃敦煌
该区荒漠的主要特点是各种戈壁广布，这是极干旱区有名的"百里大戈壁"，上面有水流的痕迹，也分布着星星点点的植被。近处的电线杆和右上角的公路让人更感戈壁的广袤。

The Wilderness of Gobi Desert—Dunhuang, Gansu
In this region, the main characteristic is the widespread Gobi desert of different kinds, known as "the Enormous Gobi Desert". In this extremely arid area, the Gobi is marked with water flowing tracks and dotted with some vegetation. The nearby telephone poles and the road in the upper right corner make more sense of the vastness of the desert.

沙漠守护神·内蒙古额济纳旗

胡杨是荒漠地区特有的珍贵森林树种,耐寒、耐旱、耐盐碱、抗风沙,有极强的生命力。胡杨对于稳定荒漠河流地带的生态平衡,防风固沙,调节绿洲气候,抑制土壤盐渍化和形成肥沃的森林土壤起到了不可或缺的作用。

Desert's Patron Goddess—Ejin Banner, Inner Mongolia
Populus euphratica is a unique precious forest species in desert areas, which has a strong vitality to resist cold, drought, salt-alkali and sand and dust storm. *Populus euphratica* has played an indispensable role in stabilizing the ecological balance in desert river zone, conserving water and fixing sands, regulating oasis climate, alleviating soil secondary-salinization and forming a fertile forest soil.

日出胡杨·内蒙古额济纳旗

日出东方,大漠苍凉。胡杨有"生一千年不死,死一千年不倒,倒一千年不朽"之说。

Populus euphratica at Sunrise—Ejin Banner, Inner Mongolia
Sun rises from the east shedding on the barren desert. It is said that *Populus euphratica* "stays alive for a thousand years, stays upright for a thousand years when it is dead and stays un-decayed for a thousand years when it fell down".

古湖盆·内蒙古额济纳旗

在这极干旱地区的古湖盆底，沙土大量沉积，大风起兮尘亦扬。这里年均8级以上大风日数超过44天，大风常伴随产生沙尘暴，年均沙尘暴次数达14次之多。毫无疑问，这里是我国沙尘暴最重要的策源地之一。

The Ancient Lake Basin—Ejin Banner, Inner Mongolia

In this extremely arid area, the ancient lake basin has serious sand deposition and dust blowing problems at the bottom. The days that wind force equals or is greater than force 8 are more than 44 days annually, along with frequent sand and dust storms, which is over 14 times each year. There is no doubt that this is one of the most important sources of sand and dust storms in our country.

1. 梭梭
   Haloxylon ammodendron

2. 盐碱滩"植被圈"
   Circle of Vegetation on Salt Marshes

3. 沙枣
   Elaeagnus angustifolia

4. 白刺和盐爪爪
   Nitraria tangutorum and *Kalidium foliatum*

5. 海韭菜
   Triglochin maritimum

6. 红砂
   Reaumuria songarica

羽毛三芒草·内蒙古乌兰布和沙漠

喜生于流动、半流动沙丘上，耐干旱、耐风蚀、耐沙埋，是固定流沙不可多得的植物。

Aristida pennata —Ulan Buh Desert, Inner Mongolia

Aristida pennata grows in mobile and semi-mobile sandy land. It has strong tolerance to the drought stress, wind erosion stress and sand burial stress and is also remarkable in tacking drifting sand.

高鼻羚羊群·甘肃武威

高鼻羚羊是我国原生最珍稀的荒漠有蹄类动物之一，曾栖息于我国甘肃、新疆一带，现已经渺无踪迹，这是人工重引入的种群。为适应干冷环境,提高嗅觉灵敏度,其鼻部特别隆大而膨起,因而得名。

Saiga tatarica Group—Wuwei, Gansu

Saiga tatarica is one of the most rare ungulate species in deserts in China, and it had been found in Gansu and Xinjiang with no trace recently. Thus, it is an artificially introduced population. In order to adapt to the cold and dry environment and improve the smell sensitivity, their noses are especially bulge, hence the name *Saiga tatarica* (high-nose antelope in Chinese).

庙海子·内蒙古巴丹吉林沙漠

茫茫巴丹吉林沙漠深处有一处神秘的湖泊，湖边有一座建于清乾隆年间的藏传佛教寺庙，因而该湖泊被称为庙海子。寺庙背靠沙山，面朝湖水，庄严肃穆，幽静典雅，庙海子永不枯竭，也不被风沙所掩埋，是巴丹吉林沙漠的地标，亦是牧民心目中神圣的殿堂。

Temple Haizi — Badan Jaran Desert, Inner Mongolia

In the middle of the vast Badain Jaran Desert, there is a mysterious lake, by which there is a Tibetan Buddhist temple built in Qing Dynasty, so it is called Temple Haizi. The temple stands on the sand hills and faces the lake, solemn, quiet and elegant, which neither dry up nor buried by sand. It is the landmark in Badan Jaran Desert and also the sacred temple in the eyes of herdsmen.

沙困黑水城·内蒙古额济纳旗

历史上党项人叫额济纳河为"黑河"或"黑水",黑水为内流河,最终流入著名的古居延海。黑水城坐落在三面临水的绿洲之中,过去这里曾经十分繁华,现在该城早已废弃,周边已经是一片荒漠。黑水城是古"丝绸之路"以北保存最完整的古城遗址,记录着这里一部凄凉的自然社会变迁史。

Khara-Khoto City Trapped in Sands — Ejin Banner, Inner Mongolia

In history, the Ejin River was called "Black River" or "Black Water". The Black water is interior river, and finally it flowed into the famous ancient Juyan Lake. Khara-Khoto city is located in the oasis which faces the water on three sides. This oasis used to be very prosperous, now it has been abandoned and surrounded by a desert. Khara-Khoto city is the most complete ancient city relics located in the north of "ancient silk road", which recording the desolate natural history of social change.

巨大的洪积扇·甘肃野马山

疏勒河从祁连山山口冲出,犹如野马脱缰,携带着大量的泥沙进入河西走廊,在此形成了一个巨大的洪积戈壁扇,扇尾是荒漠绿洲,远处是供给玉门市生活、生产用水的昌马河水库,展现了一幅西部地区人们生存环境的绝妙流程图。

Huge Diluvial Fan — Mustang Mountain, Gansu

The Shu-le River rushes out from the Qilian Mountain pass, like a runaway mustang, which carrying huge amounts of sediment into the Hexi Corridor and forming a pluvial flood Gobi fan with the desert oasis in tail. In the distance is the Changma River Reservoir supplying the domestic water and production water to Yumen city, showing the excellent flow chart of living environment of people of the western region.

大漠绿洲·甘肃敦煌

有四千多年文明史的敦煌,历来为"丝绸之路"上的重镇,其南枕气势雄伟的祁连山,西接浩瀚无垠的库姆塔格大沙漠,以莫高窟及敦煌壁画而闻名天下,是汉长城、玉门关、阳关等名城名关的所在地。祁连山来水是维系这里社会繁荣的唯一生命线,有水则人进、繁荣,缺水则沙进、衰退。

The Desert Oasis—Dunhuang, Gansu

Dunhuang has four thousand years of civilization history, traditionally known as an important city in the "silk road". The south is the majestic Qilian Mountain, the west stretches the vast Taklimakan Desert, which is famous for Mogao caves and Dunhuang frescoes and where the Han Great Wall, Yumen Pass and Yangguan City are located. Water from the Qilian Mountain is the only lifeline to maintain social prosperity here, where there is water, there is people and prosperity; where the water is in shortage, the place will slip into recession.

敦格铁路穿过流动沙漠·甘肃阿克塞

敦煌至格尔木的铁路是沟通新、青、甘、藏四省（自治区）的一条最便捷通道，它连接起兰新铁路和青藏铁路两大干线，是"丝绸之路经济带"建设的重要工程，在政治、经济、国防等各领域都具有重要意义。重要工程与沙漠、戈壁交集，这种景观在本地区并不罕见。

Dunhuang-Golmud Railway on Shifting Desert — Akesai, Gansu

The railway from Dunhuang to Golmud is the most convenient way to communicate Xinjiang, Qinghai, Tibet and Gansu provinces (autonomous regions). It connects the two main arteries of Lanzhou–Xinjiang Railway and Qinghai–Tibet Railway, which is an important project of "silk road economic belt" and plays a significant role in political, economic, national defence fields. The important projects intersect with the desert and Gobi, which is not uncommon in this region.

4

北疆盆地干旱极干旱区
The Arid and Extremely Arid Areas in the Northern Xinjiang Basin

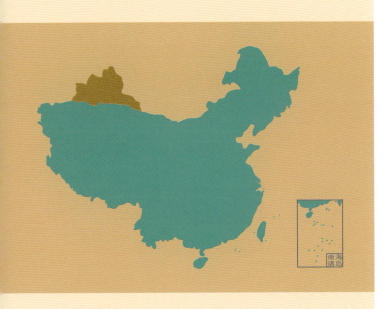

北疆盆地干旱极干旱区

该区域为中国地势第二级阶梯的西北部分，南为天山山脉，北至阿尔泰山，西至哈萨克斯坦国界，东至阿拉善高原区，属典型大陆性干旱气候，年均气温 −4～9℃，全年降水量 150～200 mm，干燥度 3.0 到 9.0 左右，四季分明。北疆荒漠四面环山，所形成的准噶尔盆地为中国第二大内陆盆地，呈不规则三角形，地势向西倾斜，北部略高于南部，西南部的艾比湖湖面 189 m，是盆地最低点。北面的阿勒泰山脉和南面的天山山脉有很多河流发源，除额尔齐斯河注入北冰洋外，玛纳斯、乌伦古等内陆河多流注盆地，潴为湖泊。盆地西部有伊犁谷地、额敏谷地和额尔齐斯谷地等缺口，使西风环流自大西洋上空携带的剩余水汽进入境内，形成一定的降水，降水可达 200～250 mm，使北疆平原区成为西北荒漠区中降水较多的地区。

准噶尔盆地中部为广阔草原和沙漠，部分为灌木及草本植物覆盖，主要为南北走向的垄岗式固定、半固定沙丘，南缘为鱼鳞状沙丘。位于盆地中央的古尔班通古特沙漠，是仅次于塔克拉玛干沙漠的中国第二大沙漠，绝大部分为固定和半固定沙丘，其面积占整个沙漠面积的 97%，固定沙丘上植被覆盖度 40%～50%，半固定沙丘达 15%～25%，为优良的冬季牧场。沙丘上广泛分布以红柳、白梭梭、梭梭、蒿属、蛇麻黄和多种一年生植物为主的荒漠植被。干旱和风是这里沙漠形成的两个主要原因，沙漠的沙物质主要来源于天山北麓各河流的冲积沙层。沙漠中最有代表性的沙丘类型是沙垄，占沙漠面积的 50% 以上，其长度从数百米至十余千米，高度自 10～50 m 不等，南高北低。这里雅丹地貌特别出众，面积大，分布广，且形状和色彩极其丰富。

区域内有鹅喉羚、蒙古野驴、普氏野马、盘羊等兽类，也有金雕、猎隼、鸳、红隼等猛禽，卡拉麦里是荒漠野生动物的天堂。

准噶尔盆地主要自然灾害有冻害和大风，盆地东部为寒潮通道，冬季为中国同纬度最冷之地。由于盆地植被覆盖度较大，虽大风天数多，沙丘移动现象却较塔里木盆地为少。由于大量引水灌溉，玛纳斯湖已经干涸，艾比湖的面积也已缩小。在草地利用方面突出的矛盾是季节不平衡和水草不平衡，随着人口数量的增长，这种压力将越来越大。保护山地森林植被，完善和恢复山地—平原—绿洲复合系统，节水和合理分配水资源，合理调整、利用天然草地，走生态保护、农牧结合、节水农业之路，实现高效、集约经营的可持续发展，是北疆荒漠区的发展对策。

（前页）五彩湾雪·新疆吉木萨尔
在卡拉麦里的戈壁荒漠中有一个五彩缤纷的世界，那就是以怪异、神秘、壮美、多彩而著称的五彩湾。千百年来几经沧桑，覆盖地表的沙石被风雨剥蚀，大雪过后，色彩缤纷的山体披上了银装。

(Previous Page) Snow in Multicolored Bay—Jimusar, Xinjiang
In the Gobi desert of Kalamaili, there is a colorful world, namely Multicolored Bay, which is well known for its strangeness, mystery, magnificence and colorfulness. For thousands of years of vicissitudes, the covered surface is corroded by the wind and rain. After the heavy snow, the colorful mountains look as if dressed in silver.

（从左至右）
垄岗式沙丘·新疆古尔班通古特沙漠
风蚀雅丹地貌·新疆奇台
干旱区典型灌木——膜果麻黄·新疆塔城
八哥群与牛群·新疆布尔津
准噶尔油田·新疆昌吉

(From Left to Right)
Strip Composite Sand Ridge — Gurbantunggut Desert, Xinjiang
The Wind Eroded Yardang Landform — Qitai, Xinjiang
Representative shrub of arid regions, *Ephedra przewalskii*—Tacheng, Xinjiang
Flocks of Crested Myna (*Acridotheres cristatellus*) and Herds of Cattle — Burqin, Xinjiang
The Oil Field in the Junggar Basin — Changji, Xinjiang

The Arid and Extremely Arid Areas in the Northern Xinjiang Basin

This area is next to Tianshan Mountains in the south and Altai Mountains in the north, bordering Kazakhstan in the west and Alxa Plateau in the east, within a typical continental arid region. It has four distinct seasons, with an annual temperature of 19-21°C, comprehensive precipitation of 150-200 mm and drought index of 3.0-9.0. The desert in north of Xinjiang is surrounded by mountains on four sides, which formed the second largest inland basin in China, in shape of irregular triangle. The terrain tilts to the west with the north slightly higher than the south, and the surface of Ebinur Lake in the southwest is the lowest point of the basin. There are many rivers in the Altay Mountain in the north and Tianshan Mountains in the south, most of which are the inland rivers, such as Manas River and Ulungur River, emptying into the basin to form lakes, except the Irtysh River, which empties into the arctic ocean. In the west of the basin, there are gaps like Yili Valley, Emin Valley and Erzius Valley enabling the westerly circulation to carry the remaining water vapor from the Atlantic into this territory and forming a certain precipitation of 200-250 mm, thus the northern plain became an area with more precipitation in the northwest deserts.

The central part of Junggar Basin is vast grassland and desert, partly covered by shrubs and herbs. It mainly consists of ridge type fixed dunes and semi-fixed dunes along the north and south directions, while the south side is scaled dunes. Located in the central basin of the Gurbantunggut Desert, it is the second largest desert in China after Taklimakan Desert. Most of the areas are fixed and semi-fixed dunes accounting for 97% of the total desert area in this region. As an excellent winter pastures, the coverage of vegetation is 40%-50% on fixed dunes and 15%-25% on the semi-fixed dunes. The dunes are widely distributed with rose willow, *Haloxylon persicum*, *Haloxylon ammodendron*, *Kobresia*, *Ephedra distachya* and small arbor tree desert vegetation dominated by a variety of therophyte plants. Drought and wind are two main reasons for the formation of this desert, and the material mainly originates from the river alluvial sand in north of Tianshan Mountains. In the desert, the most representative types of sand dunes are longitudinal dunes, which accounted for more than 50% of the desert area. Its length ranges from hundreds of meters to more than ten kilometers, height from 10 m to 50 m with the south higher than the north. The Yardang landform is particularly outstanding, with large area, wide distribution and a variety of shapes and colors.

There are *Gazella subgutturosa*, *Equus hemionus*, *Equus przewalskii*, *Argali sheep* and other beasts, also there are *Aquila chrysaetos*, *Falco cherrug*, *Buteo*, *Falco tinnunculus* and other raptors. Kalamaili is a paradise of desert wildlife.

The main natural disasters in Junggar Basin are freezing damage and strong wind. The eastern part of the basin is cold wave channel, and it is the coldest area in winter compared with the same latitude places in China. As the vegetation coverage of the basin is large, although there are many windy days, the movement of the dunes is less than that in the Tarim Basin. The Manas Lake has dried up and the area of the Ebinur Lake has shrunk since a large number of water diversion irrigation has been carried out in this region. In grassland utilization, the prominent contradiction is seasonal imbalance and water-grass imbalance. With the increase of population, there will be increasing pressure. The mountain forest protection, the improvement and restoration of the compound system in mountain plain oasis, the water saving and rational allocation of water resources, the reasonable adjustment, the utilization of natural grassland for animal husbandry, pursuing ecological protection, water-saving agriculture, so as to achieve sustainable development with high efficiency and intensive management are countermeasures to the development of northern desert region.

红色砾漠·新疆哈密

经过长期风化剥蚀的基岩碎屑物或山下坡积物，由于地面缺乏土壤，气候又十分干旱，植物稀少而形成砾石荒漠。红色砾漠不多见。

A Red Gravel Desert — Hami, Xinjiang

Hami City, Xinjiang has turned into a gravel desert because of the bedrock clast or slope wash under the hill after a long-term weathering erosion, the lack of surface soil, the arid climate, and few plants. The gravel desert, red in color, is uncommon.

大沙沟与带状沙丘·新疆阿勒泰

古尔班通古特沙漠北面的大沙沟和垄岗式带状沙丘正处于夕阳之中。准噶尔盆地中部为广阔草原和沙漠，部分为灌木及草本植物覆盖，主要为南北走向的垄岗式带状固定、半固定沙丘。

The Big Sand Gully and Banded Dunes — Altay, Xinjiang

The big sand gullies and the ridging banded dunes in the north of the Gurbantunggut Desert are under the early setting sun. The vast grassland and the desert are in the central Junggar Basin, which is partly covered by shrubs and herbs and mainly by fixed or semi-fixed dunes in the ridge and ribbon shape.

鱼鳞状沙丘组合及带状沙垄·新疆昌吉

干旱和风是这里沙漠形成的两个主要原因。古尔班通古特沙漠的沙物质主要来源于天山北麓各河流的冲积沙层，顺着强力风向，形成最具特点的大带状沙垄。古尔班通古特沙漠的沙垄占到沙漠面积的 50% 以上，其长度从数百米至十余千米。

Scale-shaped Dunes and Banded Longitudinal Sand Ridges — Changji, Xinjiang

Drought and wind are the two main causes of the desert coming into being here. The sandy material of the Gurbantunggut Desert mainly comes from the alluvial sand layer of the rivers in the northern foot of the Tianshan Mountain, and forms the most characteristic striped longitudinal dunes along the strong wind trend. The sand ridges here account for more than 50% of the whole desert area and their lengths vary from several hundred meters to over ten kilometers.

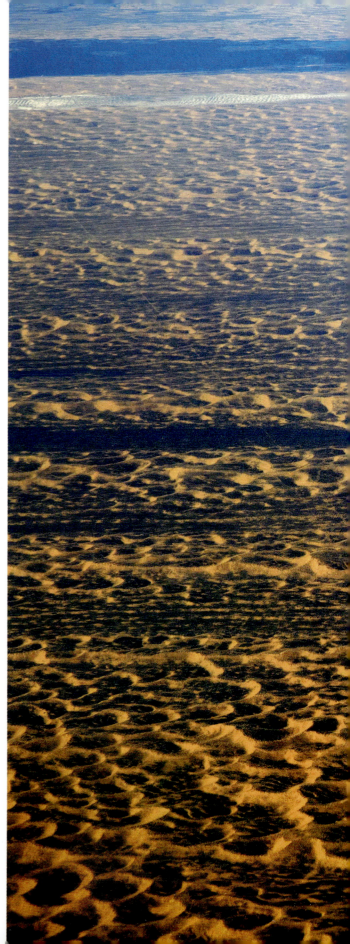

沙垄的典型形式·新疆哈密

这是普通的沙垄，只是这个沙垄简单、干净得有些出奇。

The Typical Longitudinal Dune — Hami, Xinjiang

It is a common longitudinal dune, while it is unusual for its plainness and pureness.

五彩滩的傍晚·新疆布尔津

"雅丹"原是维吾尔族语，意为陡峭的土丘。在极干旱地区的一些干涸的湖底及近坡，常因干涸而裂开，风以及暂时性流水的侵蚀，使裂隙愈来愈大，发育成许多不规则的背鲫形垄脊和宽浅沟槽，这种支离破碎的地面被称为雅丹地貌。新疆的雅丹地貌分布最多，除了南疆罗布泊和古楼兰一带的雅丹地貌外，北疆克拉玛依的"魔鬼城"、奇台的"风城"等都是典型的雅丹地貌。

The Wucai (Colorful) Beach at Dusk — Burqin, Xinjiang

"Yardang", originally a Uygur language, means the steep earth mound. Yardang landform is used to describe the fragmented ground with many irregular ridges and wide shallow trenches developing at the bottom of some dry lakes and around the slope in the extremely arid region through the erosion of wind and ephemeral drainage. It is distributed mostly in Xinjiang Autonomous Region. Apart from this landform along Lop Nor in southern Xinjiang and the ancient Loulan area, the specific landforms such as "Demon City" in Karamay and Qitai's "Wind City" in northern Xinjiang are the typical Yardang landform.

夕阳"魔鬼城"·新疆克拉玛依
这座特殊的"城堡"里,有城墙、街道、楼房、雕塑等,其形象生动、惟妙惟肖,堪称鬼斧神工。夕阳西下,如血的残阳给雅丹魔鬼城换了装,金碧辉煌中现出几分神秘、几分诡异,引人无限遐想。

"Demon City" at Sunset — Karamay, Xinjiang
In this special "castle", there are walls, streets, buildings, sculptures and so on, which can be regarded as the uncanny workmanship for their vivid images remarkably like the true. At sunset, the Demon City in the Yardang landform represents another scene which captures the imagination by adding an air of mystery to its original splendid and magnificent figure.

生态系统的多重组合 · 新疆巴里坤

在天山北坡，蓝天下的雪山、森林、沙漠、草原、湿地呈立体排列，递次展现在我们面前，那么多不同类型的生态系统居然在同一个小环境下共存，这种异常难得的大自然景观如此震撼，让人目瞪口呆、回味无穷。

Combination of Multiple Ecosystems — Balikun, Xinjiang

In the northern slope of the Tianshan Mountain, snow-covered mountains, forests, deserts, grasslands, and wetlands under the blue sky were arranged in three dimensions, unfolding before our eyes. How shocked and stunned people would be when seeing such a scarce natural wonder where so many different ecosystems coexist in the same small environment.

雪山下的胡杨林·新疆伊吾

伊吾胡杨号称是地球上树干造型最奇特的胡杨，是一片树龄最高的胡杨，也是离城市最近的胡杨，其中有六人合而不抱的大胡杨。晨光中，雪山下的胡杨林犹如驰骋在祖国北部边疆的金戈铁马，讲述着新疆古老的历史文化，讲述着中华民族抵抗外来侵略者可歌可泣的故事。

Populus euphratica Forest under the Snow-covered Mountains — Yiwu, Xinjiang

Yiwu's *Populus euphratica*, known as one with the most peculiar trunk shape on the earth, is the oldest in tree-age and the nearest from the city, including one that is so big that six people can't encircle it hand in hand. In the morning light, *Populus euphratica* trees on the snow-covered mountains are like shining spears and armoured horses galloping along the northern frontier of our motherland, representing the ancient history and culture of Xinjiang and telling the touching story of the Chinese nation against foreign invaders.

冬末聚群的公羊·新疆吉木乃

这是不同年龄的盘羊公羊聚群活动。在冬末季节发情期，公羊和母羊是分别聚群的，集群规模与栖息密度正相关。盘羊主要栖息在具有荒漠草原分布、地势相对平缓开阔的山地，在新疆主要分布在盆地的盆边或盆周，有垂直迁徙现象。盘羊的视觉、听觉和嗅觉敏锐，性情机警，稍有动静，便迅速逃遁，常以小群活动，每群数量不多。

Clustered Rams in the Late Winter — Jimunai County, Xinjiang

This is a clustered activity of male argalis at different ages. During the seasonal estrus in the late winter, rams and ewes are clustered respectively, with a positive correlation between the cluster size and habitat density. The main habitat of argali is in the mountains with desert grassland and relatively gentle terrain. It is mainly distributed along or around the basin in Xinjiang Autonomous Region for the vertical migration phenomenon there. With keen vision, hearing and olfaction, and alert disposition, argali would escape quickly at any disturbance, and they are always clustered in a small group.

(左页)外面的世界白茫茫·新疆富蕴
因为地域环境不同,新疆不同的地域里分布着不同的盘羊亚种,亚种有8～9种之多。这只盘羊在自己的地域往外看,外面是一片不熟悉的白茫茫世界。

(Opposite Page) Outside World in White Colour — Fuyun, Xinjiang
Diverse subspecies of argali, with about eight or nine kinds, are distributed in different areas in Xinjiang for the various geographical environment. This argali is looking outside of its "sphere of influence" at an unfamiliar world in white colour.

起飞瞬间·新疆卡拉麦里
棕尾鵟是一种喜欢干燥环境的猛禽,栖息于荒漠、半荒漠、草原、无树的平原和山地平原,主要以野兔、啮齿动物、蛙、蜥蜴、鸟类等为食,是荒漠生态系统食物链的顶级物种之一。

The Moment of Taking off — Kalamaili, Xinjiang
Buteo rufinus, a kind of bird preferring a dry environment, inhabits in the desert, semi-desert, grassland, tree-free plains, and mountains and plains. It is one of the top species of the food chain of the desert ecosystem, mainly with hares, rodents, frogs, lizards, birds and so on as its food.

1. 普氏野马发情·新疆卡拉麦里
   The Oestrus of Przewalski's Horse — Kalamaili, Xinjiang

2. 蒙古野驴·新疆卡拉麦里
   Equus hemionus — Kalamaili, Xinjiang

3. 大公岩羊·新疆阿尔金山
   Big Male *Pseudois nayaur* — Altun Mountain, Xinjiang

4. 天山马鹿·新疆夏尔西里
   Cervus elaphus — Xarxili, Xinjiang

齐行·新疆卡拉麦里

这是三只鹅喉羚小公羊在一起。鹅喉羚也叫长尾黄羊，属典型的荒漠、半荒漠区域生存的动物，平时常结成3～6头一起的小群生活，秋季汇集成百余只的大群做季节性迁移。

Marching Side by Side — Kalamaili, Xinjiang

This is a scene that three small male *Gazella subgutturosa* members walk together. *Gazella subgutturosa*, also called *Goitered gazelle*, is a typical animal living in the desert and semi-desert area. Small groups varying from three to five members are formed for living at normal time and big groups with over 100 members will come into being for seasonal migration in autumn.

野马奔腾·新疆卡拉麦里

放归野外的普氏野马群在自由自在地奔驰着。普氏野马原分布于中国新疆准噶尔盆地北塔山及马鬃山一带，19世纪中后期消失了。1986年，中国林业部门在新疆建立了野马繁殖研究中心，实施了"野马还乡"计划，先后从国外引进18匹野马进行繁育。21世纪开始，首次将27匹人工繁育条件下的野马放归野生环境并获得成功。

Galloping Brumbies — Kalamaili, Xinjiang

Przewalski's horses are galloping freely when coming back to the wild. They were originally distributed in Beita Mountain and Mazong Mountain of the Junggar Basin, Xinjiang Autonomous Region, China, but they disappeared from the second half of the 19th century. In 1986, the Chinese forestry department established the Brumby Reproduction Research Center in Xinjiang, and implemented the "Brumby Reintroduction" Program, with 18 brumbies introduced from abroad for breeding. At the beginning of the 21st century, it was the first time that 27 brumbies through the artificial breeding had been reintroduced to the wild successfully.

北水南调·新疆昌吉

新疆北水南调工程引水渠跨越古尔班通古特沙漠。

Diverting Water from North to South — Changji, Xinjiang

The canal of the North-to-South Water Diversion Project of Xinjiang goes across the Gurbantunggut Desert.

沙漠水库·新疆昌吉

引额尔齐斯河水给准噶尔盆地西部、南部输水，是一项重大的跨流域、长距离的北水南调水利工程。它的建设不仅可以解决北疆地区油田勘探开发、沿线农业综合开发和城市生活用水的水资源问题，还将有力促进相关工业的建设，推动经济发展和社会稳定。

Desert Reservoir — Changji, Xinjiang

The North-to-South Water Diversion Project is an important inter-basin and long-distance one, diverting water from Irtysh River to the western and southern parts of the Junggar Basin. Its construction can not only solve the water supply problem for the exploration and development of the oil field in the northern Xinjiang region, and the agricultural comprehensive development of agriculture and urban life along the route, but also will effectively promote the construction of related industries, the economic development and the social stability.

巨大的虹吸工程·新疆阿勒泰
跨越古尔班通古特沙漠大沙沟的水利虹吸工程和沙漠公路。

Huge Syphonage Project — Altay, Xinjiang
The Water Syphonage Project and the desert expressway go across the Gurbantunggut Desert.

未来的 G7 高速·新疆伊吾
京新高速公路（编号 G7），起点为北京，终点为乌鲁木齐，其中额济纳至哈密段穿过中蒙边界地区的大戈壁无人区。京新高速的全面建成通车，将为"一路一带"的建设发展做出重大的贡献。

The G7 Expressway—Yiwu, Xinjiang
Beijing-Urumchi Expressway (abbreviated as Jin-Xin Expressway, numbered as G7) starts form Beijing to Urumchi, Xinjiang Autonomous Region, with a section built from Ejin City to Kumul City that goes across a big desert on the China-Mongolia border region without anybody living there. The completion of Jin-Xin Expressway will make significant contribution to the development of Belt and Road Initiatives.

5 南疆盆地极干旱区
The Extremely Arid Areas in the Southern Xinjiang Basin

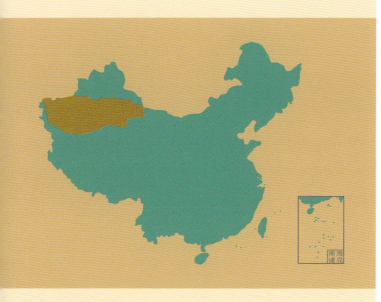

南疆盆地极干旱区

该区域为中国地势第二阶梯的西部分，北为天山山脉，南为昆仑山—阿尔金山脉，东达罗布泊洼地东缘，西为帕米尔高原，大地貌上包括塔里木盆地和吐鲁番—哈密盆地。经历新生代喜马拉雅造山运动，塔里木盆地便形成大型坳陷盆地，接受沉积。地表覆盖巨厚的第四纪风积、冲积、洪积与湖积沉积物及部分基岩风化物。

该区域属暖温带极干旱气候，区内年均降水量小于100 mm，干燥度5.0以上，有的地方甚至超过100。南疆盆地沙砾物质来自古河湖相沉积物、近代河流冲积物、山前洪积物、第三第四纪岩层风化物。沙丘形态以流动沙丘为主，其面积占沙丘面积的80%以上。

塔克拉玛干沙漠位于新疆南疆的塔里木盆地中心，是中国最大、世界第二大沙漠，同时亦是世界最大的流动沙漠。整个沙漠东西长约1000 km，南北宽约400 km，面积达33万 km²。平均年降水不超过100 mm，最低只有4～5 mm；而平均蒸发量却高达2500～3400 mm。库姆塔格沙漠位于塔里木盆地的东缘，是中国第六大沙漠，同时亦是中国第四大流动沙漠，东西长约280 km，南北宽约120 km，总面积约2.28万平 km²。两大沙漠都具有典型的雅丹、风棱石、风蚀坑等风蚀地貌以及格状沙丘、新月形沙丘、蜂窝状沙丘、金字塔形沙丘、线状沙丘等沙丘类型和复合型沙丘类型，库姆塔格沙漠还有独特的羽毛状沙丘。

用塔里木盆地与准噶尔盆地相比，降水和山地河流的流入，前者都比后者少。该区植被群落为暖温带荒漠群落，主要由驼绒藜、戈壁针茅、梭梭、泡泡刺、蒿属、猪毛菜、假木贼等组成。覆盖度低，一般小于15%。该区动物极端稀少。只是在沙漠边缘地区，在有水草的古代和现代河谷及三角洲，动物才较为多样。在开阔地带可见成群的羚羊，在河谷和盆地灌木丛中有马鹿、野骆驼、野猪、狼、狐狸、猞猁、北山羊、塔里木兔等。

由于这里自然环境恶劣，在河流沿岸和下游的天然绿洲都处于退化状态。灌溉农田用水已经在20世纪80年代就感到十分紧张，河流下游河道缺水十分严重，天然绿洲逐渐退化。所以，必须从保护天然绿洲的水分生态平衡出发，宏观调整和控制人工绿洲的水资源利用，实施退耕还林还草和退水，保障荒漠绿洲的供水，才能保证南疆盆地生态环境改善和社会经济的可持续发展。

（前页）大沙垄·新疆塔里木盆地
塔克拉玛干沙漠维吾尔语意为"进去出不来"，又称"死亡之海"，位于新疆南疆的塔里木盆地中心，是中国最大、世界第二大沙漠，同时亦是世界最大的流动沙漠。由于气候极其干旱，整个沙漠受南北两个盛行风向的交叉影响，风沙活动十分频繁而剧烈，沙丘类型复杂多样，流动沙丘占80%以上。

(Previous Page) The Great Ridge — The Tarim Basin, Xinjiang
The Taklimakan Desert means "no return" in Uygur language, so it is also called "the sea of death". It is located in the central Tarim Basin in southern Xinjiang, the largest one in China and the second largest one as well as the largest shifting desert in the world. For the extremely arid climate, it has frequent and severe wind-sand activities under the cross influence of two prevailing winds from south and north. So there are dunes in various and complex shapes, with the shifting dunes accounting for more than 80%.

（从左至右）
新月形沙丘组合·新疆喀什
岁月的雅丹·新疆巴音郭楞
梭梭与红柳·新疆阿克苏
夕阳双驼·新疆巴音郭楞
盐湖和盐田·新疆哈密
(From Left to Right)
Combination of Crescent Dunes — Kashi, Xinjiang
Yardang Landform over the Years — Bayingolin, Xinjiang
Haloxylon ammodendron and Rose Willow — Aksu, Xinjiang
Two Camels in the Setting Sun — Bayingolin, Xinjiang
Salt Lake and Salt Field — Hami, Xinjiang

The Extremely Arid Areas in the Southern Xinjiang Basin

It goes northward to Tianshan Mountains Basin, southward to Kunlun-Altun Mountains, eastward to the eastern edge of Lop Nor Depression, westward to the Pamir Plateau. The landform includes the Tarim Basin and the Turpan-Hami Basin. After the Cenozoic Himalayan orogeny, the Tarim Basin formed a large depression basin, receiving sedimentation. The surface covers a lot of eolian, alluvial, diluvial, and lacustrine deposits and some bedrock weathering materials during the quaternary period.

It is in the extremely arid climate at the warm temperate zone, an average of less than 100 mm of precipitation and a dryness of 5.0 or more with even over 100 in some places. The gravel materials in the southern Xinjiang Basin are sediments of ancient rivers and lakes, modern river alluviums, diluviums before mountains, and rocky weathered products during the Tertiary and Quaternary periods. The sand dunes are mainly shifting dunes whose area accounts for more than 80% of the whole.

The Taklimakan Desert, located in the central Tarim Basin in southern Xinjiang, is the largest one in China and the second largest one as well as the largest shifting desert in the world. It is about 1000 km long from east to west, and 400 km wide from south to north, which covers about 330,000 km^2. Its average annual precipitation is less than 100 mm, with the lowest of 4-5 mm, while its average annual evaporation is up to 2500-3400 mm. The Kumtag Desert, located in the eastern margin of the Tarim Basin, is the sixth largest one and the fourth shifting desert in China. The desert is about 280 km long from east to west, and 120 km wide from south to north, which covers about 22800 km^2. The two large deserts have typical kinds of wind-erosion landforms such as Yardang landform, ventifact, and blowout, and single dunes in various shapes such as trellis, crescent, honeycomb, pyramid, and linearity, and compound dunes, with the feather-shaped dune as the distinctive type in the latter desert.

Comparing the Tarim Basin with the Junggar Basin, we can find the former is inferior to the latter in precipitation and the number of jointing rivers from mountains. Its plant community is a desert type at the warm temperate zone, with *Ceratoides latens*, *Stipa gobiea*, *Haloxylon ammodendron*, *Nitraria sphaerocarpa*, *Artemisia*, *Salsola collina*, and anabasis and so on as the main components. Its vegetation coverage is low, generally less than 15%. With extremely scarce animals, it has more diverse animals only in the margin of the desert and the ancient and modern valleys and deltas with waterweeds. Groups of antelope can be seen in the open area, and many more species, such as red deer, wild camels, wild boars, wolves, foxes, lynxes, *Cabra ibex* and hare, can be found in the valley and basin-margin bushes.

Because of the poor natural environment here, the natural oases along the river and the lower river are in degradation. Irrigation water was in shortage in the 1980s, a serious lack of water occurred in the lower reaches of the river, and natural oases gradually degraded. Therefore, based on protecting the ecological balance of the natural oases, we should improve water resources utilization through the macro adjustment and control of artificial oases, and implement projects of converting cultivated land into forests and grassland, so that the improvement of the ecological environment in the southern Xinjiang Basin and social and economic sustainable development will come true.

航拍金字塔形沙丘·新疆塔克拉玛干沙漠
Aerial Photos of Pyramid-shaped Dunes — The Taklimakan Desert, Xinjiang

金字塔形沙丘·新疆塔克拉玛干沙漠
塔克拉玛干沙漠的流动沙丘占沙丘总面积的 80% 以上，由于整个沙漠受南北两个盛行风向的交叉影响，造成复杂的环流系统，风沙活动十分频繁而剧烈，使沙丘类型复杂多样。金字塔形沙丘是一种具有明显棱面的高大沙丘，一般有 3 或 4 个棱面，是各种方向的风相互作用而成的。

Pyramid-shaped Dunes — The Taklimakan Desert, Xinjiang
With the shifting dunes accounting for over 80% of the whole, the Taklimakan Desert has frequent and severe wind-sand activities and a complex circulation system under the cross influence of two prevailing winds from south and north. So there are dunes in various and complex shapes. The pyramid-shaped dunes, a high one always with obvious 3–4 planes, are formed through the mutual interaction of winds in all directions.

复合型沙丘·新疆塔克拉玛干沙漠
由两种不同的基本类型沙丘组合而成的大沙丘叫复合型沙丘,有复合新月形沙丘和复合沙丘链等形态。

Compound Dunes — The Taklimakan Desert, Xinjiang
The compound dunes refer to the great one combined with two dunes in different basic types, which have diverse forms such as the compound crescent dunes and compound dune chains.

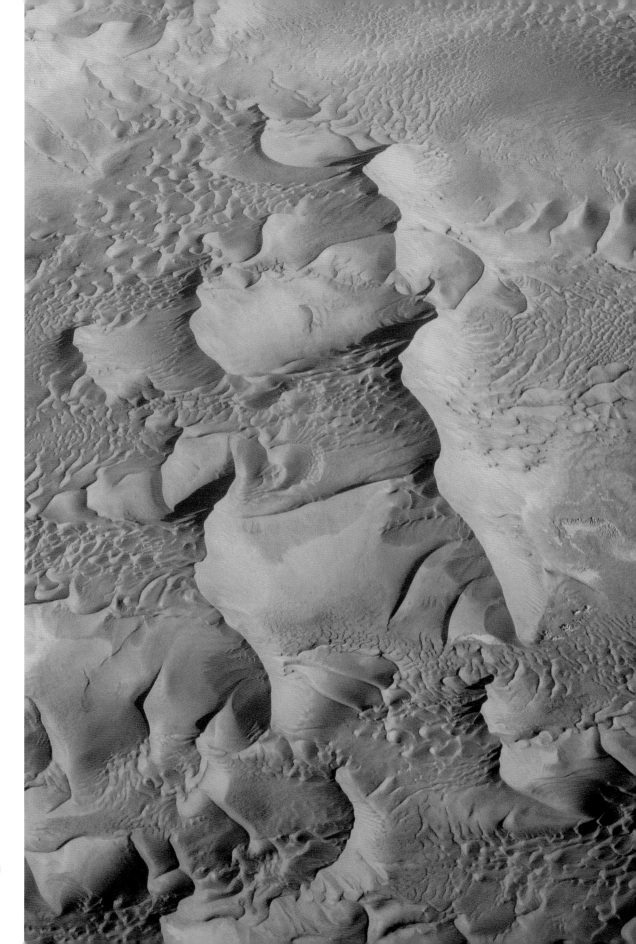

航拍复合型沙丘·新疆塔克拉玛干沙漠
Aerial Photos of Compound Dunes — The Taklimakan Desert, Xinjiang

羽毛状沙丘的"羽管"和"羽"·新疆库姆塔格沙漠

库姆塔格沙漠南依阿尔金山，西北毗邻罗布泊，北达阿奇克谷地，东抵敦煌鸣沙山，为中国第六大沙漠。在沙漠的北部有一片中国唯一的羽毛状沙丘，羽毛的"羽管"由一串单个的新月形沙丘前后相连而成，羽毛的"羽"为与之几近垂直相交并低矮一些的一条条平行延伸的沙埂，从空中俯瞰，就像一片羽毛轻轻地覆盖在阿尔金山北麓的洪积扇上面。

Feather-shaped Dunes — The Kumtag Desert, Xinjiang

With Altun Mountain in its north and Lop Nor in its northwest, the Kumatag Desert goes northward to the Aqik Valley and eastward to the Mingsha Mountain, Dunhuang City, Gansu Province. It is the sixth largest desert in China. In its northern part, there is a field filled with feather-shaped dunes. These feather tracts are made of a string of crescent dunes connected one after another, with many lower long sand ridges almost intersecting perpendicularly, extending in parallel. Seen from the air, it is like a feather gently covering on the diluvial fan in the north of the Altun Mountain. These are the feather tracts of the feather-shaped dunes and sand ridges in the photo.

1

2

3

4

1. 戈壁上面的水蚀沟·新疆喀什
   The Water-eroded Ditches on the Gobi Desert — Kashgar, Xinjiang

3. 干裂的湖底沉积·新疆吐鲁番
   The Dry Deposit at the Bottom of the Lake — Turpan, Xinjiang

2. 沙丘间湿地·新疆阿克苏
   A Wetland between Dunes — Aksu, Xinjiang

4. 戈壁—砾石滩·新疆喀什
   Gobi Desert-Boulder Beach — Kashgar, Xinjiang

盆边戈壁·新疆和田

塔克拉玛干沙漠四周，天山在北，昆仑山在南，帕米尔高原在西，东面逐渐过渡，直到罗布泊沼盆。在盆地南面和西面，在沙漠和山脉之间，有很多由卵石碎屑沉积物构成的成片戈壁坡地。

The Gobi Desert on the Edge of a Basin — Hotan, Xinjiang

With Tianshan Mountain in its north, Kunlun Mountain in its south, the Taklimakan Desert transits gradually from the Pamir Plateau in its west to the Lop Nor swampy basin in its east. There are many sloping fields made of detritus and deposit from the gravel in the area between its northern and western part and between deserts and ranges.

153

1

2

3

4

1. 盐角草
   Salicornia europaea

3. 沙蓬
   Agriophyllum squarrosum

2. 骆驼刺
   Alhagi sparsifolia

4. 猪毛菜
   Salsola collina

天山下的猫头刺·新疆哈密
猫头刺为旱生小灌木，多生长在砾石堆、沙地上，为荒漠草原的标志性植物。

The *Oxytropis aciphylla* under Tianshan Mountain — Hami, Xinjiang
The *Oxytropis aciphylla*, a little xerophyte bush, is a typical plant in the desert steppe, growing mostly on the gravel fillet and the sandy soil.

活跃的盘羊·新疆巴音郭楞
在新疆几乎处处都活跃着盘羊，只是在不同的地域、不同的亚种而已。它们能在悬崖峭壁上奔跑跳跃，来去自如，而且极耐渴，能几天不喝水，冬天无水就吃雪。盘羊食性较广，分布区的各种植物均能食用。

Two Vigorous Argali — Bayingolin, Xinjiang
There are argali almost everywhere in Xinjiang, with different subspecies in different regions. They can run and jump on the cliffs, coming and going as they like, and they can endure the extremely thirsty, without drinking water for a few days. They eat a wide range of foods including all kinds of plants in their distribution areas.

石鸡妈妈和它的孩子们·新疆库尔勒
石鸡栖息于低山丘陵地带的岩石坡和沙石坡上以及草原、荒漠等地区，性喜集群，以草本植物和灌木的嫩叶、浆果、种子、苔藓和昆虫等为食。雏鸟早成性，孵出后不久即能跟随亲鸟活动。

A Mother and Her Offspring of the *Alectoris chukar* — Korla, Xinjiang
The *Alectoris chukar* inhabits on the rocky slopes and gravel slopes of the low hilly areas, as well as steppe, desert and other areas. They are in fond of being in groups in nature, and their foods are various such as the tender leaves of bush, the berries, the seeds, the mosses and the insects. The young ones can follow their kinsfolks in movement soon after being hatched out.

曾经的瀚海·新疆罗布泊

罗布泊位于新疆塔里木盆地东北部的若羌县境内，这里地势低洼，是新疆南部塔里木盆地的聚水中心，曾经河流交织，湖泊星罗棋布。塔里木河、孔雀河、车尔臣河、疏勒河等汇集于此，西北侧的楼兰城为著名"丝绸之路"的咽喉。罗布泊曾为中国第二大咸水湖。之后，由于气候变迁及人类水利工程的重大影响，导致上述诸河上游来水减少，1960年代塔里木河下游断流，到1972年，罗布泊完全干涸。现在湖心地区遍布着湖水退却、湖盆干涸后形成的坚硬而尖利的盐壳。

A Vast Ocean Used to Be—Lop Nor, Xinjiang

Lop Nor, a low place within Charkhlik County in the north-eastern part of the Tarim Basin in Xinjiang Autonomous Region, is the center of the basin, which was once filled with many rivers and lakes. Many rivers converge there, such as the Tarim River, the Qarqan River and the Shule River, and the Loulan City in the northwest is the key link of the "Silk Road". Lop Nor was once the second largest saltwater lake of China. However, with the reducing water in the upper reaches of the above-mentioned rivers under the influence of climate change and the water conservancy projects, the lower reaches of Tarim River set off in 1960s and Lop Nor dried up completely in 1972. Its central area is filled with hard and sharp salt shells developed after the water receded and the lake basin dried.

靠近鄯善城的高大沙丘·新疆鄯善
处于沙漠和雅丹地貌之间的绿洲就是人们居住的地方，这里狭小的绿洲是靠有限的水资源维持的。这在新疆很有代表性。

High Dunes near Shanshan County — Shanshan, Xinjiang
People live in the oasis between the desert and the area of Yardang landform, which is supplied by the limited water resources. This is typical in Xinjiang Autonomous Region.

葡萄沟·新疆鄯善

沙漠与雅丹地貌夹持下的葡萄沟，河道旁是杨树组成的农田防护林和晾干葡萄的晾房。有水就有生命，有水才有绿色，在干旱和半干旱地区，水比什么都重要。

The Grape Valley—Shanshan, Xinjiang

The Grape Valley between the desert and the area of Yardang landform, has the farmland shelterbelt made of the poplars and rooms for drying grapes along the stream channel. Water is the most important in the arid and semi-arid areas. Therefore, where there is water, there is life and green.

6

**青藏高原
高寒干旱极干旱区**
The Alpine Arid and Extremely Arid Areas in the Qinghai-Tibet Plateau

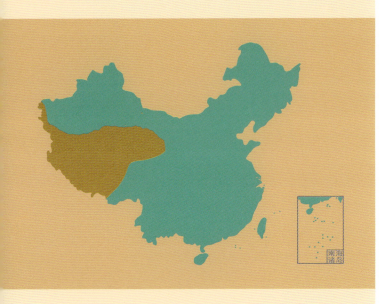

青藏高原高寒干旱极干旱区

这里属于中国地势第一阶梯的青藏高原，范围为昆仑山—阿尔金山—祁连山以南，喜马拉雅山以北，日月山—巴颜喀拉山—聂拉降巴雪山以西的区域，西界为喀喇昆仑山。高寒与干旱的气候背景是本区的荒漠不同于其他干旱区域之处。本区的柴达木—共和盆地是断陷作用形成的盆地，海拔3000 m左右。在喜马拉雅山北麓，由于印度洋暖湿气流产生的焚风效应，加剧了气候的旱化，干燥度达10.0以上。雅鲁藏布江上中游、拉萨河周边流动沙丘广布，甚至翻山越岭。该区还分布有世界上海拔最高的库木库里沙漠，海拔在3900～4700 m。

这里属高原大陆性气候，太阳辐射强烈，日照多，气温低，日较差大，年变化小，积温少，光照充足，冬季干冷漫长、大风多，夏季温凉多雨、冰雹多，四季不明，全年无夏。干燥度由2.0递增到20.0左右。

区域地处大陆腹地，受到高大山脉的阻挡，使得暖湿空气难以到达，降水稀少，而日照充足又使蒸发量相对较大，因此区域内河流大都径流量较小且流程较短，大多以冰雪融水为主要补给水源。区域内除雅鲁藏布江、象泉河外多属于内流水系，地势低洼处盐湖与沼泽广布，形成为数众多的半咸水、咸水湖，如著名的青海湖、纳木错、哈拉湖等。

植物种以适应寒冷干旱的生态条件为主，代表植物有小蒿草、紫花针茅、固沙草、西藏蒿、垫状驼绒藜等。这里是高寒野生动物的天堂，藏羚羊、藏野驴、野牦牛、雪豹、藏原羚、普氏原羚、白唇鹿以及高山兀鹫、胡兀鹫、金雕等活跃在这片广阔的高原上。

由于地理、历史等原因，该区经济发展落后，生态环境比较脆弱，加之人们对区域内的环境生态价值缺乏深远的认识，在一定程度上导致了对资源盲目的和不合理的开发利用，使本来就十分脆弱且极不稳定的高原环境承受着越来越沉重的压力。诸如雪线上升，冰川退缩，土地沙化，水源枯竭，植被退化，草地沙化，水土流失及泥石流灾害加剧等现象在该区域尤显突出。草地的沙漠化加剧了高原气候的干旱和风沙侵蚀，因此，实行严格的国土资源保护政策和有效措施，禁止过牧和开垦，保护水资源，防治荒漠化，使土地能够休养生息，逐步恢复良好的生态环境才是该区生态环境保护和建设的根本途径。

（前页）青藏高原北缘·青海海北
这里是连绵千里的祁连山脉，祁连山海拔4000 m以上终年积雪，与干旱的柴达木盆地间仅有逾1000 m高差。

(Previous Page) Northern Margin of the Qinghai-Tibet Plateau — Haibei, Qinghai
Stretching for thousands of *li* here, Qilian Mountains are covered with snow all the time for years at an elevation of over 4000 m. The height difference just exceeds 1000 m between them and the Qaidam Basin.

（从左至右）
布伦口湖畔越岭的沙丘·新疆克孜勒苏柯尔克孜
扎嘎沟砾石坡·西藏珠穆朗玛峰下
沙丘下的沙棘·青海青海湖
奔跑的藏羚羊·青海可可西里
牦牛运输队·青海海西

(From Left to Right)
Sand Dune beside the Bulunkou Lake and the Mountains — Kirghiz of Kizilsu, Xinjiang
Zhagagou Gravel Slope — at the foot of Qomolangma Mountain, Tibet
Sea-buckthorn under the Sand Dune — Qinghai Lake, Qinghai
The Running Tibetan Antelope — Hoh Xil, Qinghai
Yak Transportation Team — Haixi, Qinghai

The Alpine Arid and Extremely Arid Areas in the Qinghai-Tibet Plateau

It is an area in the northern Qinghai-Tibet Plateau, with the Kunlun-Altun-Qilian mountain range in its north, the Himalaya Mountains in its south, the Riyue-Bayankala mountain range in its east and Karakorum mountain range in its west. The deserts in this region are distinct from that of other regions with the alpine arid and extremely arid climate. The Qaidam-Gonghe Basin had been developed under the impact of taphrogeny, with an elevation of about 3000 m. From the margin to the center of the Qaidam Basin, the volcanic gravel fan, the alluvial-flooding sandy plain, the lacustrine alluvial silt clay soil plain, the lacustrine silt plain are distributed in a circular shape, changing regularly. And there are widespread salt lakes and marshes in low-lying areas.

For the plateau continental climate, there are strong solar radiation, much sunshine, low temperature, large daily difference, small annual variation, low accumulated temperature, and adequate light. It is cold and dry in the long winter with frequent strong winds and it is warm and cool in summer, with much rain and hail. The changes of four seasons are not obvious, with no real summer throughout the year. The dryness degree increases from 2.0 to 20.0 or so.

The area is located in the hinterland of the mainland, blocked by the high mountains, making the warm and humid air difficult to reach, scarce precipitation and abundant sunshine make the evaporation relatively large, so the runoff and the process flow of the river in the region are relatively small and short, with snow melt water as its main source of water supply. Most of the river systems in the area belong to closed drainage, as the river water pours into the depression, a large number of salt lake formed, such as the famous Qinghai Lake, Nam Lake and Hala Lake.

The plant species are dominated by those adapted to the cold and arid ecological conditions, represented by small wormwood, *Stipa purpurea*, *Orinus thoroldii*, *Tibetan artemisia*, and *Ceratoides compacta*. This vast highland is a paradise for such alpine wildlife as *Tibetan antelope*, Tibetan wild donkey, wild yak, snow leopard, Tibetan gazelle, *Procapra przewalskii*, white-lipped deer and Himalayan vultures, *Gypaetus barbatus* and golden eagle.

Economic development in this region is backward and its ecological environment is fragile due to geographical and historical reasons, which makes it one of the weakest regions in economic strength in China. On top of that, the lack of foresight on the environmental and ecological values of the region has led to the blind and unreasonable development and utilization of resources to a certain extent, making the pressure on the plateau environment which is already very fragile and extremely unstable increasingly heavy. Snow line rising, glacial recession, land desertification, exhaustion of water source, vegetation degradation, grassland desertification, water and soil erosion and the intensification of debris flow disasters in the region were particularly prominent. The desertification of grassland exacerbates the aridity of the plateau climate and wind erosion, therefore, the basic solution to protect and improve ecological environment of this region is to implement strict policies and effective measures on land resources protection, prohibit overgrazing and reclamation, protect water resources and prevent desertification, so as to recuperate the land and gradually restore a good ecological environment.

青海湖畔沙山雪·青海海晏

作为中国第一大湖泊的青海湖，周边有成片的流动沙丘。其东岸沙丘是在干旱气候下形成的大规模风沙堆积，沙丘高大、连绵不断。而西岸沙丘则是近二十几年来才形成的湖滨沙丘，沙丘边缘逐年向青海湖水面逼近，目前其规模已成为仅次于东岸的第二大风沙堆积区。在高寒干旱条件下，人们大面积垦荒、过牧是沙丘形成和不断扩张的最重要原因。

Snow on Sand Hills beside Qinghai Lake — Haiyan, Qinghai

As the largest lake in China, Qinghai Lake is surrounded by patches of shifting dunes. The dunes on its east coast are formed by large-scale aeolian sediments in the arid climate, which is tall and continuous. The dunes on its west coast are the lakeside dunes formed in the past 20 years. The edge of the dunes is approaching the Qinghai Lake year by year. At present, second to the east coast, its scale has become the second largest wind and sand accumulation area. The most important reason of the dunes formation and continuous expansion is large-scale reclamation and overgrazing under the cold and arid conditions.

丹霞地貌下的黄河·青海贵德

由于黄河水下切和喜马拉雅山造山运动隆升，红色砂砾岩层经过千万年流水的侵蚀和风的雕凿，便形成了千姿百态的耸岩峭壁。河水的清澈、大天鹅的洁白和红色的环境相映成趣。

The Yellow River under Danxia Landform — Guide, Qinghai

As the undercut of the Yellow River and uplift from the orogenic movement of the Himalayas, after thousands of years of erosion and wind-carving, red gravel rock formation formed a variety of rock cliffs. The clean river, the pure white whooper swan and the red surroundings contrast finely with each other.

（右页）昆仑山深处戈壁·新疆塔什库尔干

本区最西端塔什库尔干古城旁边的砾石滩。在高原高寒的昆仑山深处，有大量的戈壁分布。

(Opposite Page) Gobi in the Bowels of Kunlun Mountains — Tashkurghan, Xinjiang

The gravel bank is beside the ancient city of Tashkurghan in the westernmost tip of this area. In the highlands of the bowels of Kunlun Mountains, there distributes vast Gobi.

湖畔风云·青海青海湖

这里的沙丘逐年向青海湖水面入侵，而高原的气候恶劣多变，空气扰动特别厉害，狂风、龙卷风常常形成且助纣为虐。这里大量将草地变为农地的做法已经开始受到了大自然的惩罚。

Beautiful Scenery beside the Lake — Qinghai Lake, Qinghai

The dunes here has been invading into the Qinghai Lake year by year, since the climate of the plateau is very harsh and changeable and the air disturbance specially is severe, fierce wind and tornado are often formed which aggravate the condition. The practice of turning huge areas of grassland into farmland has begun to be punished by the nature.

希夏邦马峰下的流动沙丘·西藏日喀则
Shifting Sand Dune at the Foot of Shisha Pangma Mountain — Shigatse, Tibet

希夏邦马峰下的戈壁·西藏日喀则

希夏邦马峰是喜马拉雅山脉中唯一一座全部位于中国境内海拔在 8000 m 以上的高峰。由于印度洋暖湿气流被喜马拉雅山脉阻挡产生的焚风效应，喜马拉雅山脉北麓极其干旱，年轻地质结构不稳定，山体不断剥离产生大量的碎石，因而北麓有大片的戈壁分布。

Gobi at the Foot of Shisha Pangma Mountain — Shigatse, Tibet

Shisha Pangma Mountain is the only peak among its 8000 m-tall counterparts in the Himalayas that stands completely within China's territory. As a result of the Foehn wind effect through which the warm and humid air stream from the Indian Ocean was blocked by the Himalayas, the northern sides of the mountains are often very dry. Besides, given that the geological structure of this region is relatively young and unstable, rocks tend to break apart and fall, leading in result to huge amounts of rubbles, which explains the existence of vast Gobis at the northern slope.

岗嘎大戈壁及高大沙丘·西藏定日
沿着岗嘎大戈壁向南顺坡而上，就是珠穆朗玛峰、卓奥友峰、洛子峰等海拔 8000 m 以上山峰之间的多条巨大冰川。戈壁的产生和雪山冰川融水形成的洪积扇密切相关。在岗嘎戈壁中间还有一处高大的流动沙丘。戈壁沙漠干旱的灰黄色和白雪、蓝天形成了强烈的对比。

The Kongga Greater Gobi and Tall Dunes — Tingri, Tibet
Moving upward from the south of the Kongga Greater Gobi, one will come across several huge glaciers intersected by Qomolangma Mountain, Cho Oyo Mountain and Lhotse Mountain, all of which are over 8000 m in altitude. The existence of the Gobi is closely tied with the proluvium fan generated by the melting glaciers. At the center of the Kongga Greater Gobi is one huge shifting dune. The yellowish arid Gobi desert contrasts sharply with its surrounding white snow and the blue sky.

沙质河漫滩和翻山越岭的沙丘·西藏雅鲁藏布江中游
在雅鲁藏布江河谷强劲风力的作用下，河漫滩中的沙挟持裸露的草地、农地上更多的沙源四处肆虐，掩埋村庄和农田，甚至翻山越岭到处流窜。

Sandy Floodplains and Shifting Dunes — the Middle Reaches of the Yarlung Zangbo River
Carried by the strong winds along the Yarlung Zangbo River valley, sands originating from the floodplains, which are constantly supplemented with more sands from exposed grasslands and farmlands, ravage over villages and farmlands. In serious cases, they can even move across mountain ranges to get into neighboring watersheds.

泥漠·青海哈拉湖

泥漠主要分布于荒漠中较低洼处,雨季河流夹带的泥沙在低洼的湖沼中沉积,旱季时强烈蒸发,水量减少,湖沼干涸,土地龟裂,经长期反复作用后即形成泥漠。本区哈拉湖周边以及柴达木盆地有大量泥漠。

Mud Desert — Lake O'Hara, Qinghai

The mud desert is mainly distributed in the lower depression of the desert. The sediment in the rainy season is deposited in the low-lying lakes and marshes. During the dry season, the water evaporates intensively, the water yield is reduced, the lakes are dried up and the land is cracked, and the mud desert is formed after a long period of repeated actions. There are a large number of mud deserts around the area of Hala Lake and the Qaidam Basin.

盐漠·青海柴达木

盐漠又称盐碱地，为盐水浸渍的泥漠，分布于荒漠的低洼部分。盐分易于吸收水分引起膨胀，所以长期处于潮湿状态，干涸时可形成龟裂地，仅能生长少数盐生植物，是荒漠中土壤最贫瘠的类型。柴达木盆地低洼处盐湖与沼泽广布，有大量这样的荒漠类型。"柴达木"为蒙古语，意为"盐泽"。

Salt Desert — Qaidam Basin, Qinghai

Salt desert, also known as saline and alkaline land, mud desert immersed by saline water, is distributed in the low-lying parts of the desert. Salt expands for absorbing moisture easily, so after in a damp state for a long time, cracked land is formed when dried up, only a small number of halophytes can grow, so the salt desert is the most barren soil in the desert. The salt lakes and swamps are widespread in the low-lying part of the Qaidam Basin, and there are a large number of deserts like this. "Qaidam" is from Mongolian language, meaning "salt marsh".

1

2

3

4

1. 垫状植物和鼠洞
   Cushion Plants and Mouse Cave

2. 地衣
   Lichens

3. 大黄
   Rheum sp.

4. 苞叶雪莲
   Saussurea obvallata

骆驼刺·青海格尔木

骆驼刺为内陆干旱地区的一种草本植物，根系非常发达，甚至能够从沙漠和戈壁 20 m 深处吸取地下水分和营养。其茎上长着刺状的坚硬小绿叶，是戈壁滩和沙漠中骆驼能吃的植物，故名"骆驼刺"。其存在与生长对于维护极为脆弱的荒漠生态环境有着极其重要的生态价值。

Alhagi sparsifolia — Golmud, Qinghai

Alhagi sparsifolia is a kind of herbaceous plant in inland arid area, whose roots are well developed and even can absorb underground moisture and nutrients from the desert and the 20 m depth of Gobi. As the stem with little spinulose hard green leaves, it is the plant that camels can eat in Gobi and the desert, hence named "Camel Thorn" in Chinese. Its existence and growth have an extremely important ecological value for the maintenance of very fragile desert ecological environment.

领地之战·青海海南

面对强大的高山兀鹫，乌鸦（小嘴乌鸦）对侵犯自己领地的入侵者毫不畏惧，前前后后、左左右右不断地发起攻击。作为大型猛禽的高山兀鹫竟然也招架不住乌鸦的频频驱赶，最终落荒而逃。

The Battle of Territory — Hainan, Qinghai

Facing the invasion from the strong Himalayan vulture, the crow (*Corvus corone*) is fearless to the invaders invading its territory, and continues to fight against the invader from all directions. Under that condition, even Himalayan vulture, a large raptor, cannot withstand the frequently expelling from the crow, and ultimately fled away.

鸟中之王·青海阿尔金山

金雕为鸟中之王,以其凶猛的外观和敏捷有力的飞行而著名,成鸟的翼展平均超过 2 m,体长则可达 1 m,其腿爪上全部都有羽毛覆盖,以大中型的鸟类和中小型兽类为食,最高分布海拔高度可到 4000 m 以上,是我国分布最广的大型猛禽之一。

The King of Birds — Altun Mountain, Qinghai

As the king of birds, the golden eagle is famous for its ferocious appearance as well as agile and powerful flying. The adult birds' wingspan stretches more than 2 meters on average, and their bodies are up to 1 meter in length, with the legs and claws all covered with feathers. They feed on large-and-medium-sized birds and small-and-medium-sized beasts, and the highest altitude of their distribution can be more than 4000 m. They are the kind of big raptors with the widest distribution and the largest population.

碱蓬边的鹅喉羚·青海德令哈

一群鹅喉羚在碱蓬地处观望。鹅喉羚属典型的荒漠、半荒漠动物。红色的碱蓬是一种盐生植物，耐盐碱、耐贫瘠。由于茎叶肉质，叶内贮有大量的水分，故能忍受暂时的干旱。碱蓬在碱湖周围和盐碱滩地上多星散或群集生长，可形成纯群落。

Gazella subgutturosa beside *Suaeda glauca* — Delingha City, Qinghai

A group of *Gazella subgutturosa* are watching at the land of *Suaeda glauca*, and they are typical desert and semi-desert animals. As a kind of halophytes, red *Suaeda glauca* can endure the saline-alkaline and barren, and they can tolerate temporary drought because their fleshy stem leaves can store a lot of water. They grow around the alkali lake and in the land of salt marsh, sparsely or collectively, so a pure community can be formed.

1. 在洞口探风的鼠兔
   Pika Testing the Waters at the Entrance of Cave

2. 嗜食腐肉的胡兀鹫
   Lammergeier Addicted to Carrion

3. 栖息在鼠兔洞里的一对蟾蜍
   Frog Inhabiting in the Cave of Pika

4. 世界上分布海拔最高的雉类之一——雪鸡
   One of the Pheasant Species Distributed on the Highest Altitude in the World — Snow Cock

可爱的小藏羚羊·西藏羌塘

藏羚羊为中国特有物种，群居，国家一级重点保护野生动物。曾因为一段时期盗猎、偷猎现象频发，它们的种群数量在 90 年代迅速下降，后来由于国家和社会强有力的保护行动，数量目前已经明显回升。

Small and Lovely Tibetan Antelope—Qiangtang, Tibet
As a unique species in China, Tibetan antelope living in groups is the wildlife under the first class state protection. Because of frequent illegal hunting and poaching for a time, the number of their population had declined rapidly in the 1990s, but has now risen obviously thanks to the vigorous protection efforts made jointly by the government and the society.

登高健将·新疆昆仑山

北山羊栖息于海拔 3500 ~ 6000 m 的高原裸岩和山腰碎石嶙峋的地带，非常善于攀登和跳跃，蹄子极为坚实，能够自如地在险峻的乱石之间纵情奔驰，是羊中的登高健将。

Climbing Athlete — Kunlun Mountain, Xinjiang

Inhabiting in plateau bare rocks at the altitude of 3500 — 6000 m and areas at the mountainside with gravels, *Capra sibirica* is very good at climbing and jumping. With extremely solid hooves, they are able to run freely through steep rocks, so they are regarded as the climbing athlete among the goats.

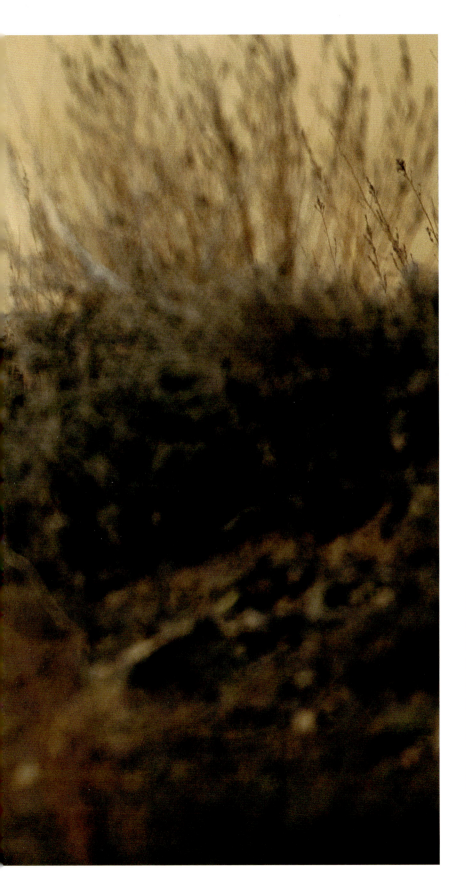

雪山之王·青海格尔木

雪豹是一种美丽而濒危的猫科动物，生活在世界最高海拔的雪域高原，雄踞在冰峰雪岭之上。它是整个山地生物多样性的旗舰物种，是健康山地生态系统的指示器，被称为"雪山之王"。

King of Snow Mountain—Golmud, Qinghai

The snow leopards are beautiful but endangered felines. Known as the "King of Snow Mountain", they live in the highest elevation of snow-covered plateau and are flagship species of mountain biodiversity and indicators of a healthy mountain ecosystem.

褐背拟地鸦·青海海南

在青藏高原的草原上常见褐背拟地鸦白天进出鼠兔的洞穴，鸟、鼠兔同居一穴，鼠兔在里面打洞，鸟儿为其站岗放哨。鼠兔可借助鸟类的惊鸣来报警，鸟可利用洞穴躲避太阳的强烈辐射或暴风与冰雹，这种生物现象被称作"鸟鼠（兔）同穴"。

Pseudopodoces humilis — Hainan, Qinghai

It is common to see the *Pseudopodoces humilis* in and out of pika's burrows in the grassland of Qinghai-Tibet Plateau. Birds and pikas live together. Pika burrows caves inside, while the bird stands sentry for it, and sometimes pecks parasites for the pikas. Birds' cry can alarm pikas of danger, while the birds can avoid the intense sun radiation, storm and hail by aid of caves. This biological phenomenon is called "Birds and Pika Sharing the Same Cave".

大漠生灵 · 青海德令哈

藏野驴是典型的青藏高原荒漠动物，多栖息于海拔 3000～5000 m 的高原亚寒带，喜欢排成一路纵队，鱼贯而行。其具有极强的耐力，既能耐冷耐热，又能耐饥耐渴，并且具有敏锐的视觉、听觉和嗅觉，由于"好奇心"所致，常常追随经过的人和汽车。

Desert Creatures — Delingha, Qinghai

Tibetan wild donkey is a typical animal in Qinghai-Tibet Plateau desert, which inhabits plateau sub frigid zones at altitude of 3000–5000 m. They love proceeding like a school of fishes, one after another in a single file. They have extremely strong endurance, for they can not only bear cold and heat but also bear the hunger and thirsty. At the same time, they have a keen vision, hearing and smell. It often follows the passing people and cars because of their "curiosity".

争雄·青海天峻

普氏原羚是一种典型的在荒漠与半荒漠环境生活的哺乳动物，也是世界上最濒危的有蹄类动物，其角尖相向内弯，末端形成相对钩曲，现只分布于中国青海湖周围。发情期的公羊为了配偶权而争斗，连一贯性情温和的普氏原羚雄性之间的争夺也异常激烈。

Competing for Female—Tianjun, Qinghai
Przewalski's gazelle is a kind of typical mammal in desert and semi-desert environment, and is also the world's most endangered ungulate animal for it only distributes around Qinghai Lake in China. Its two horns bend inwards towards each other, and curved hooks are formed at the end of the horns. The estrous rams always fight for the spouse; competitions between the male Przewalski's gazelles are fierce even though they are always moderate in temper.

发情·青海天峻
处于发情期间，刚刚被雄性追逐后才停下来喘气的雌性普氏原羚。

Rut—Tianjun, Qinghai
In the period of estrous, the female Przewalski's gazelle stopped for breath after the male's chasing.

喜马拉雅旱獭·青海玉树

一对喜马拉雅旱獭在打闹。喜马拉雅旱獭喜欢穴居、群居，为青藏高原最常见、体形最大的啮齿动物。由于天敌的种类较多，所以它的性情极为机警，视觉、听觉都很敏锐，每当遇有狼、狐、雕、鹰、艾鼬等天敌进入领地时，就直立起来发出尖锐的鸣叫。

Marmots Himalayana —Yushu, Qinghai

A pair of marmots himalayana are in play. Being the most common and the hugest rodent, the marmots himalayana likes to live in caves and groups. Owing to a large number of natural enemies, it has a quick wit and the keen sense of sight and sense of hearing. It will straighten itself and shrill when such natrual enemies as wolves, foxes, eagles and fitchews enter its territory.

攻击前的警示·青海海西

野牦牛是典型的高寒动物，为青藏高原特有种，极耐寒，性凶猛善战，四肢强壮，身被长毛，群居。性情凶狠暴戾的孤牛常会主动攻击在它面前经过的各种对象。野牦牛发起攻击时首先会竖起尾巴示警。

Warning before Attack—Haixi, Qinghai

Wild yak is a typical alpine animal, which is endemic to the Tibet Plateau. It is very hardy, ferocious with strong limbs and long furs, and is gregarious. Solitary cruel and fierce cattle often launch active attack against various objects in front of them. Before attack, the wild yak will first give a warning with its raised tail.

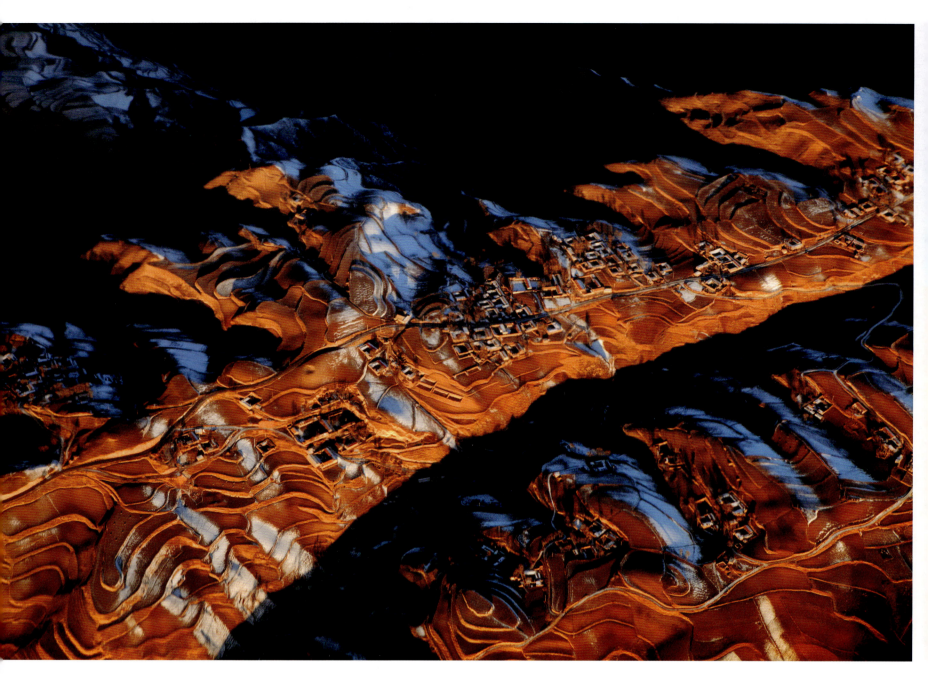

高原人家·青海海东
高寒干旱荒漠区的农地和民居浸润在晨光中。

People in Plateau—Haidong, Qinghai
Farmland and houses in the arid and cold desert areas are soaked in morning lights.

野放的家骆驼·青海柴达木

这里有不少野外放养的双峰家骆驼，它们自由自在地在荒漠中生活，以致有的人在没有看到真正野骆驼的时候，会将它们误认为是野骆驼。

Field Stocked Home Camels—Qaidam, Qinghai

There are many free-ranging two-humped camels in the desert, which are mistakenly thought to be wild camels by someone who has never seen the real wild ones.

沙海牧羊归·青海刚察
回归的羊群在流动的沙丘上，画出了一幅对比生动的流动路线图。
The Returning Flock in the Sea of Sand—Gangcha, Qinghai
The returning flock draws a contrasting and flowing map on the shifting dunes.

早上好！·青海海南
清晨，岩羊上到佛塔上舔食盐碱，与藏传佛教的喇嘛相遇。他们如同老朋友相见一样，双方相致问候。
Good morning!—Hainan, Qinghai
In the morning, a Tibetan Buddhist lama meets with a bharal that climbs on the pagoda base to lick salt. They greet each other like old friends.

生态思考
Ecological Reflections

相比起地球上的其他生态系统，荒漠生态系统显得异常脆弱，一旦被破坏影响范围极大。在世界范围内，绝大部分干旱、半干旱区为荒漠、草场，人们的土地利用方式更适宜游牧或者低强度的利用。而在干旱、半干旱区过牧，在边缘区定牧或者进行农业开垦往往会导致这一地区土地荒漠化的发生。《联合国千年生态系统评估》中谈到，荒漠化的生态影响、社会影响及政治影响并不仅限于荒漠化地区，荒漠化的生态影响可达数千千米以外。发生在中国西北地区的沙尘暴可以影响到北京、朝鲜半岛、日本甚至北美地区；东非及撒哈拉的沙尘暴可以影响到北美及加勒比海地区。因荒漠化而产生难民，导致人口迁徙，必然加剧其他地方的压力，进而影响全球社会、政治及经济稳定。荒漠化，特别是沙化问题，是全球性的生态环境问题，影响着全球三分之二的国家和地区、五分之一人口的生存和发展。

从最基本的人生需求讲，对于很多生活在干旱、半干旱区的人们而言，基本生活物质主要源自初级生物的生产产品，荒漠生态系统通过其服务功能为人类提供粮食、肉、奶、燃料及建筑材料等。过度放牧或者土地开垦导致荒漠生态系统服务功能下降，或需要更多的水肥投入。人口的增加、承包或短期土地利用政策往往导致使用者过度利用土地资源，诱发一些非持续利用现象的发生，从而导致土地的退化，即荒漠化。土地退化导致了土地生产力下降，人们就要继续通过增加开垦来维持生物总产量，从而使得荒漠化进一步加剧。更有荒漠化导致动物、植物多样性下降，导致初级生产力下降并引起碳汇能力下降和地表辐射增加，这些都会引起全球气候变化。

因此我们可以说，荒漠地区土地利用的变化既是荒漠生态系统变化的结果，又是其变化的原因。我们总是看到，在荒漠区，人与荒漠之间总是纠缠在沙进人退、人进沙退之中；总是纠缠在土地或退化、或进化（恢复）的局面之中。因此，防治荒漠化就是保护和恢复荒漠生态系统的服务功能，而生态系统服务功能的恢复可以通过人与生态系统相互作用来实现。我们不搞"人定胜天"、也不盲目"向沙漠进军"，我们提倡"师法自然"，就是要按照自然规律去做。我们更不能在荒漠化日益威胁的情况下，束手无策、无所作为。

中国是世界上荒漠化最为严重的国家之一，1994—1996年全国第一次荒漠化和沙化监测结果显示，全国流动沙丘面积42.72万km^2，固定及半固定沙地46.30万km^2，戈壁及风蚀劣地71.14万km^2，其他14.14万km^2。八大沙漠、四大沙地是我国主要沙源地，全国沙化土地面积为168.9万km^2，中国可能发生荒漠化的范围为331.7万km^2。

我国土地沙化扩展速度70年代每年1560km^2，80年代为2100km^2，90年代达2460km^2，21世纪初达到3436km^2，相当于每年损失一个中等县的土地面积。据统计，60年代特大沙尘暴在我国发生过8次，70年代发生过13次，80年代发生过14次，而90年代发生过20多次，并且波及的范围愈来愈广，造成的损失愈来愈重。每年因土地沙化造成的直接经济损失超过540亿元人民币。荒漠化是中华民族永续发展的民生之痛、民心之痛。

防治荒漠化迫在眉睫，这个问题引起了党中央、国务院的高度重视，及时出台并实施了一系列行之有效的政策和措施，在各级党委政府的领导下，经过荒漠区广大人民群众多年的艰苦奋斗和不懈的努力，我国荒漠化和沙化整体扩展趋势得到了初步遏制。我国沙漠化土地由1995年至1999年的年均扩展3436km^2转变为2000年至2004年的年均净减少1283km^2，开始出现了拐点。

2016年第五次全国荒漠化和沙化监测结果更让人眼前一亮，我国荒漠化和沙化状况有明显好转，呈现整体遏制、持续缩减、功能增强、成效明显的良好态势。全国荒漠化土地面积减少到261.16万km^2，年均减少2424km^2；沙化土地减少到172.12万km^2，年均减少1980km^2。我国荒漠化土地和沙化土地面积自2004年出现拐点以来，荒漠化和沙化面积持续减少，沙化逆转速度加快，沙尘天气次数减少，强度减弱，影响范围减少，保持了我国荒漠化、沙化土地连续15年"双减少"。究其原因有以下几方面。

一是实施了以生态建设为主的发展战略，"三北防护林工程""京津风沙源治理""天然林资源保护""野生动植物保护及自然保护区建设工程"等重点工程以及草原保护和建设、水土保持、内陆河流流域综合治理等项目成效明显，为实现沙化土地整体好转发挥了重要作用。

二是构建了以《中华人民共和国防沙治沙法》为主的法律法规和政策体系。2000年以来，在原有环境保护的法律法规基础上，国家相继制定实施了《中华人民共和国防沙治沙法》《中华人民共和国环境影响评价法》《中华人民共和国森林法实施条例》等法律法规，修订完善了《中华人民共和国草原法》，出台了《省级政府防沙治沙目标责任考核办法》，制定了《沙化土地封禁保护修复制度方案》等一系列惠农惠牧治沙政策措施，有效地保障了防沙治沙工作的顺利进行。

三是坚持科学防治。全面落实荒漠生态保护红线，遵循自然规律，严格保护好荒漠生态系统、荒漠天然植被，促进自然植被休养生息。因地制宜，采用生物、农业和工程措施综合治理，结合人工恢复与人工促进自然修复。同时，加大现有如草方格、低覆盖度防沙治沙等多项适用技术和模式的推广和应用力度。

我们自豪地看到，中国这些年防治荒漠化的努力已经大见成效，荒漠化、沙化土地连续15年"双减少"的成绩得到了国际社会的广泛赞誉。联合国第十七届可持续发展大会指出，中国荒漠化防治处于世界领先地位。2017年，我国将举办《联合国防治荒漠化公约》第13次缔约方大会，这是国际环境方面的公约缔约国大会首次在中国召开，有着非常重大的意义。这次大会的主题是"携手防治荒漠化，共谋人类福祉"，主要任务是围绕联合国确立的"到2030年实现全球土地退化零增长"的重大目标，各国如何携手应对荒漠化的挑战。而这些年来，中国已经初步走出了一条具有中国特色的防治荒漠化的道路，形成了法律、政策、规划、考核以及工程建设、科技支撑、监测预警、履约与国际合作体系组成的防治荒漠化综合系统，为推动"一路一带"沿线国家防治荒漠化贡献了"中国方案"，为根治荒漠化这个"地球癌症"开出了"中国药方"，为实现全球土地退化零增长提供了"中国模式"。

Compared with other ecosystems on the Earth, desert ecosystems are extremely fragile, so once they are destroyed, the negative impacts would be far-reaching. Most of the arid and semi-arid areas in the world are deserts and grasslands, and are more suitable for nomadic or low intensity utilization inland use patterns. Over-grazing in the arid and semi-arid areas, grazing or agricultural reclamation in the border areas will often lead to desertification in this area. According to the *United Nations Millennium Ecosystem Assessment*, the ecological, social and political impacts of desertification are not only restricted within the desertified regions, but also may extend to areas thousands kilometers beyond. Sand and dust storms in northwestern China can affect Beijing, the Korean Peninsula, Japan, and even North America; sand and dust storms in East Africa and Sahara can affect North America and the Caribbean. Refugees fleeing from desertification result in unregulated migration, which will inevitably exacerbate the pressures on other places, hence pose serious consequences on social, political and economic stability of the world. Desertification, especially sandification, is a global ecological and environmental problem, affecting the survival and development of 1/5 population in 2/3 of the world's countries and regions.

For many people living in the arid and semi-arid areas, their essential needs for survival are mainly derived from the production of bio-products, and desert ecosystems make up the primary sources from which they get their grains, meat, milk, fuel and construction materials. Over-grazing or land reclamation leads to the decline of the service function of desert ecosystems, or alternatively, more water and fertilizer inputs are needed to meet their demands. Population growth, poorly-designed policies for short- and long-term land use often lead in consequence to over-exploitation of land resources and unsustainable manners of development, which in turn cause land degradation and desertification. Land degradation has led to declines in the productivity of lands. As a result, in order to obtain the total production that are needed for survival, the only solution people can resort to will be to increase the area of lands that are reclaimed for farming, making desertification even worse. Desertification leads to a decline in animal and plant diversities, resulting in decreases in both the primary productivity and carbon sequestration capacity, as well as in increased radiation from land surface. All these can be contributing factors for global climate change.

Therefore, we can say that the change of land use in desert areas is not only the result, but also the cause of the change of desert ecosystems. Hence, we can see that in the desert area, there are always entanglements between man and desert—people forge ahead so that sand retreats, and vice versa. This explains why people in desert areas are constantly caught up in a dilemma, with human being and nature alternatively gaining the upper hand in the long and arduous process of desertification combating; and people always entangle in land degradation, or land evolution (recovery) situation. Therefore, to a certain degree, the purpose of combating desertification is the protection and restoration of ecosystems services, which can only be achieved through mutually complementing interaction between human and ecosystems. Neither shall we adhering to the pretentious belief that "man will prevail over nature", nor do we blindly launching wars "to conquer the deserts", rather, we need to advocate to the fundamental principle of "imitating following the natural course", that is, to guide our actions with the inherent laws of nature. Faced by the ever worsening desertification, we cannot afford to just stand by and do nothing.

China is listed among countries that are most seriously inflicted by the problem of desertification. According to the first nation-wide survey on desertification carried out between 1994 and 1996, there are 427.2 thousand km^2 of sand dune areas, 463 thousand km^2 of fixed and semi-fixed sandy land, 711.4 thousand km^2 of Gobi and eroded ground, and 141.4 thousand km^2 of other desertified areas. The eight major deserts and four major sandy lands are the main sources of sand and dust storms that have rampaged across the country over the past years. The area of desertified lands in China covers 1.689 million km^2, which is still expanding at an average rate of 2460 km^2 each year. The size of desertification-liable areas in China is about 3.317 million km^2, 2.622 million km^2 among which are already suffering from desertification.

The annual expanding rates of desertified lands in China was 1560 km^2 in the 1970s, 2100 km^2 in the 1980s, and 2460 km^2 in the 1990s respectively, even reaching 3436 km^2 at the beginning of the 21st century, almost equal to the size of a medium-size county. According to statistics, catastrophic sand and dust storms in China occurred 8 times in the 1960s, 13 times in the 1970s, 14 times in the 1980s, and more than 20 times in the 1990s, causing increasingly heavier losses to ever wider areas. The direct economic losses caused by desertification each year exceed 54 billion RMB. Desertification is the pain in people's heart and of their livelihood in the sustainable development of the Chinese nation.

The imminent situation of the prevention and control of desertification caused high attention of the CPC (Communist Party of China) Central Committee and the State Council who promptly issued and implemented a series of effective policies and measures. Under the leadership of CPC committees and governments at all levels, and through the arduous and unremitting efforts of the people in the desert areas, the overall expansion trend of desertification and sandification in China has been preliminarily curbed. China's desertification land changed from an average annual expanding rate of 3436 km^2 between 1995 and 1999 to an annual net decrease of 1283 km^2 between 2000 and 2004, marking a turning point in the endeavor.

Results from the fifth national survey on desertification and sandification in 2016 are even more promising, showing that the overall situation in China has been improved significantly. A desirable situation is now in place. As the overall deteriorating trend has been effectively checked, the size of desertified lands is steadily declining, with notable progresses made in enhancing the eco-functions of recovered lands. The area of desertified lands reduced to 2611.6 thousand km^2, with an annual average decrease of 2424 km^2; the sandification area reduced to 1721.2 thousand km^2, with an average annual decrease of 1980 km^2. Since the turning point in 2004, desertification and sandification area in China continued to decrease. The number of dust-ridden days, the intensity, and the scope of sand and dust storm-inflicted areas have all been cut down notably. The trend of "double decreases", namely, decrease in both desertification and sandification, has been maintained for 15 consecutive years. The reasons are as follows.

First, we have implemented a developmental strategy that focused on ecological improvement, including the implementation of a series of key national programs, such as "Three North Shelterbelt Program", "Sand and Dust Storm Source Control Program in Vicinity of Beijing and Tianjin", "Natural Forest Resources Protection Program", and "Wildlife Protection and Nature Reserve Development Program". Remarkable achievements have been made in efforts like the protection and development of grassland, soil and water conservation, and comprehensive treatment of inland river basins. All these have played important roles in achieving overall improvement of desertified lands.

Second, a complete legal and policy system featuring *Law of the People's Republic of China on Prevention and Control of Desertification* has been put in place. Since 2000, on the basis of the existing laws and regulations on environmental protection, the government has formulated and promulgated the *Law of the People's Republic of China on Prevention and Control of Desertification*, *Law of the People's Republic of China on Environmental Impact Assessment*, *Regulations on the Implementation of the Forestry Law of the People's Republic of China* and other laws and regulations, amended and improved the *Law of the People's Republic of China on Grasslands*, and issued *Measures for the Assessment of Responsibility for Desertification Prevention and Control of the Provincial Government*, formulated the *Scheme for Enclosing Desertified Land for Protection* and *Natural Rehabilitation* and other policies and measures for desertification control in a bid to benefit agriculture and animal husbandry, which effectively guarantee the smooth implementation of desertification prevention and control efforts.

Third, the principle of scientific control has been adhered to. The red lining policy of the ecological protection on desertified land has been fully implemented, the laws of nature strictly abided by, the natural vegetation in deserts protected, and natural vegetation rehabilitation promoted. In accordance with local conditions, comprehensive controls with biological, agricultural and engineering measures have been adopted, combined with artificial recovery and promotion of natural restoration. At the same time, promotion and application of the existing technologies and patterns such as grass grids and low coverage of the sand control have been enhanced.

We are proud to see that China has achieved great progress in desertification control in these years, and achieve the "double decreases" of desertified and sandified land in China for 15 consecutive years, which has been widely praised by the world. The 17th Session of the United Nations Commission on Sustainable Development pointed out that China's desertification control is in the leading position around the globe. In 2017, China will be hosting the 13th Session of the Conference of the Parties to the UNCCD. This is the first time for China to host this grand international event, and therefore it is of great significance. The theme of the conference is "combating desertification for the wellbeing of people". On basis of the UN goal for "Land Degradation Neutrality (LDN) by 2030", participants will look into the issues of how countries can work closely to cope with the challenges of desertification. Over the years, China has pioneered a Chinese way for preventing and controlling desertification, and has brought into existence a comprehensive system that covers legal, policy, planning, performance evaluation as well as engineering construction, technical support, monitoring and early warning, convention implementation and international cooperation in combating desertification. China has contributed its "Chinese Proposals" for countries along the "The Belt and Road" to combat desertification; China has come up with a "Chinese Prescription" for coping with desertification—the "cancer of the earth"; and China has provided a "China Model" for achieving global land degradation neutrality.

主要威胁和挑战
Major Threats and Challenges

1. 气候变暖，干旱加剧

荒漠是干旱气候的产物，全球气候变暖导致干旱加剧、冰川退缩、土地沙化加重。研究表明，若大气中二氧化碳增加一倍，会使气候变化加剧，导致土地沙化面积增加17%。青藏高原冰川末端在1976年至2006年平均退缩速度为每年5 m左右，2004年至2006年退缩速度达到每年7.8 m，并表现出近期加速后退的态势。高寒草甸正以每年近8万亩（1亩=1/15 hm²）的速度消失，致使荒漠化范围扩大。干旱半干旱地区短缺的水资源在时空上分布不均，干旱缺水引发了湿地萎缩、河流断流、草场退化、土地沙化、盐渍化、地下水位下降、生物多样性锐减等生态危机。图中正在融化的八一冰川是我国第二大内流河——黑河的源头。

1. Warmer Climate and Intensifying Droughts

Deserts are the results of sustained dry weather. Global warming leads to intensified drought, glacier recession and aggravation of land desertification. Studies show that when the CO_2 content in the atmosphere doubles, the size of land desertification caused by climate change will increase by 17%. In the period between 1976 through 2006, glaciers in Qinghai-Tibet plateau have been recessing at an average annual rate of 5 m, even reaching 7.8 m for the years between 2004 to 2006. To make it worse, the recent trend is still accelerating. Alpine meadow is disappearing at an annual rate of nearly 80 thousand mu (5333 ha), resulting in the expansion of desertification. The water resources in arid and semi-arid areas, which are already in shortage, are unevenly distributed in time and space. The drought causes wetlands shrinkage, river cutoff, grassland degradation, land desertification, salinization, groundwater level decline, the loss of biodiversity and other ecological crises. The melting Bayi Glaciers in the following picture are the source of China's second largest continental river—Heihe River.

干旱加剧 冰川融化·甘肃祁连山八一冰川
Intensifying Drought and Melting Glaciers—Bayi Glaciers, Qilian Mountain, Gansu

风沙掩埋房舍·甘肃武威
Houses Buried underneath Sands — Wuwei, Gansu

2. 荒漠化加剧，自然灾害频发

目前，我国有大约 2.4 万个村庄和城镇受风沙危害，受荒漠化影响的人口达 4 亿多人。21 世纪初民勤县因为土地沙化，使得 2 万多农牧民被迫迁移他乡。塔克拉玛干沙漠周边的民丰、皮山、策勒等地，近 40 年来县城几次搬家。荒漠生态系统不稳定必然带来和加剧自然灾害的不断发生，而且愈演愈烈。

2. Drastic Desertification and Frequent Natural Disasters

At present, there are about 24 thousand villages and towns in China suffering from sand and dust storm hazards, and the number of people affected by desertification is more than 400 million. Over 20 thousand farmers and herdsmen in Minqin County have been forced to move to other place because of land desertification in the early 21st century. County seats close to the Taklimakan Desert, like Minfeng, Pishan and Qira, have been relocated several times over the last 4 decades. The instability of desert ecosystems will inevitably lead to and increase the occurrence of natural disasters which becomes more and more severe.

过度放牧·甘肃祁连山
Overgrazing — Qilian Mountain, Gansu

3. 不合理开发、开垦，过度放牧

工业化、城镇化过程中，不顾荒漠生态保护而无序开发的现象屡禁不止，到处开矿，建设用地的扩大开发不断蚕食和破坏着原有的荒漠生态系统。无序发展畜牧业，牲畜数量大大超过草地、沙地的牲畜承载力，使草场破坏、原有植被盖度减退甚至消失，沙地、草地更加裸露，土地沙化、风沙加剧，生态系统遭受破坏、甚至最终失去了自我修复的能力。

3. Unreasonable Exploitation, Reclamation, and Overgrazing

In the course of industrialization and urbanization, the phenomenon of unplanned exploitation regardless of desert ecological protections is still unchecked. Blind economic development activities, such as random mining, increased use of lands for construction land, and sprawling into sandy regions in pursuit of additional land resources for the sake of agricultural/urban growth, are constantly eroding into and destroying existing desert ecosystems. Some industrial and mining enterprises, in order to evade administrative regulations, deliberately exploit lands resources through breaking them into smaller plots. Disorderly development of animal husbandry, unregulated increases in the number of livestock regardless of the carrying capacity of grasslands and sandy grasslands, all these have resulted in either total destruction or degradation of lands. Deprived of the protection of vegetation on them, sandy lands are increasingly exposed to erosion of winds, which in the long run leaves the ecosystems incapable of self-recovery from damages.

水到尽头·甘肃河西走廊
The End of River — the Hexi Corridor, Gansu

4. 水资源不合理利用

在水资源使用方面浪费无序，到处截留水源、大水漫灌庄稼、大量抽取地下水、污水回灌乱放等水资源不合理利用现象在荒漠地区表现相当严重。罗布泊在蒙语中是"汇入多水之湖"，历史上曾拥有2万km² 水面，但由于上游来水减少以致断流，于20世纪70年代干涸，湖底盐壳隆起、沙化严重，使之变成死亡之海。黑河断流有使居延海变成第二个罗布泊之险。湖泊干涸，湖底沉淀的、失水的泥盐粉尘便是沙尘暴最佳的材料供给地、策源地。

4. Irrational Use of Water Resources

Irrational use of water resources is quite serious in desert area. For instance, disorderly use of water resources, unregulated practices in diverting watercourses, flooding irrigation of crops, pumping large amounts of groundwater, and sewage recharge or random discharge, all these still exist quite extensively in desert regions in China. Lop Nor, whose water surface used to extend for 20000 km² in history and hence named (meaning "A Lake with Numerous Affluxes" in Mongolian), dried up in 1970s due to the upstream runoff reduction. The uplift of the salt crust in the lake's bottom and severe desertification make it a sea of death. With water in Heihe River running at alarmingly low level, risks for the Juyan Lake being reduced to a second Lop Nor is very high. Sedimentary and dehydrated muddy salt dust at the bottom of the lake makes up "ideal" sources for sand and dust storms to rise.

被猎枪伤害的大天鹅·保护区救护中心
A Wounded Whooper Swan — Rescuing Center of a Nature Reserve

5. 滥捕乱猎，乱采滥挖

为了经济利益，一些地方滥捕乱猎鹅喉羚、猎隼、金雕、野兔等野生动物，乱采滥挖肉苁蓉、锁阳、甘草、发菜等野生植物的现象十分严重，一些很不容易长成的灌木，甚至草本植物，被樵采、破坏。野生动植物的破坏，打破了原来荒漠生态系统的稳定和平衡，使本来就相当脆弱的生态系统向退化、恶化方向发展，破坏容易恢复难。

5. Overhunting, Poaching and Extensive Digging

In order to pursue economic interests, overhunting and poaching of goitred gazelles, sakers, golden eagles, hares and other wild animals goes rampant in some places. In addition, extensive digging of cistanche, *Cynomorium* spp., licorice, *Nostoc flagelliforme* and other wild plants is also causing serious damages to some highly susceptible shrubs, even herbs. The damage of wildlife breaks the stability and balance of existing ecosystems, making the already fragile ecosystem degrading and deteriorating even further. Destruction is easy, but recovery is difficult.

6. 网围栏对于动物迁徙的影响

草原、荒漠草原、沙地，凡是有植被的地方，大部分都被无数的、横七竖八的网围栏分割成小块小块的独立王国。以这种方式发展畜牧业，不仅仅使草原、荒漠植被无法轮牧修养生息，也违背了野生动物迁徙的天然习性，严重地阻断了野生动物的迁徙通道，致使岩羊、鹅喉羚、高鼻羚羊、普氏原羚等有蹄类动物，甚至鸟类的活动受到相当限制，饿死、撞死、铁丝网挂死的现象时有发生。从 2003 年到 2012 年，9 年的"围栏效应"，已经导致新疆北部鹅喉羚种群数量下降了 30% 以上。

6. The Negative Impacts of Fences on Animal Migration

Most of vegetation places, desert grasslands or sandy lands, were often divided into smaller plots by countless and disorganized railing nets and fences. This practice in animal husbandry not only makes it hardly possible for the vegetation to rehabilitate through rotating, but also goes against the natural migratory habits of animals. More seriously, it blocked the migratory corridors of wild animals, like the blue sheep, *gazella subgutturosa*, saigas, Przewalski's gazelles and other hoofed animal, and even birds activities are seriously restricted. What's worse, the animals are killed, starved, hung sometimes on the fences. During the 9 years ranging from 2003 through 2012, *gazella subgutturosa* population in northern Xinjiang declined by over 30% as a result of what is known as the "Fence Effect".

撞在铁丝网上的鸟·内蒙古呼伦贝尔沙地
Birds Caught in Wire Nets — the Hulunbuir Sandy Land, Inner Mongolia

铁丝网中求生存的普氏原羚·青海湖畔
A Struggling Przewalski's Gazelle Caught in Wire Nets — beside the Qinghai Lake, Qinghai

主要措施和成就

1. 顶层设计，科学治沙

顶层设计的不断完善，是中国保护荒漠、防沙治沙得以精准发力的根本保障。《中华人民共和国防沙治沙法》《中华人民共和国野生动物保护法》《中华人民共和国自然保护区管理条例》《全国防沙治沙规划》等一系列法律法规和规章制度的相继出台，支撑起防沙治沙的法律法规体系、工程建设体系、科研与技术推广体系、监测预警体系。科学技术是精准治沙的第一推动力，抗旱造林、固沙压沙、低覆盖度治沙等治理技术不断进步，极大地提高了治沙成效。特别值得一提的是，将废弃的麦秆、谷草呈方格状铺在沙丘上，在每个草方格里孕育或者栽上耐旱的沙生植物，这种方法就地取材、成本低廉、效果明显，这项中国独创的草方格治沙被誉为"世界奇迹"。

1. Top-level Design and Scientific Desertification Control

The continuous improvement of the top-level design is a guarantee for China to implement targeted measures for desert conservation and combating desertification. Laws and regulations like *Law of the People's Republic of China on Prevention and Control of Desertification*, *Wildlife Protection Law of the People's Republic of China*, *Regulations of the People's Republic of China on the Management of Nature Reserves*, *National Plan for the Prevention and Control of Desertification* were carried out one after another, which support the law system, engineering construction system, scientific research and technology extension system and monitoring and early warning system for prevention and control of desertification. Science and technology are the first driving force for targeted desertification control. The continuous improvement of such techniques as drought resistant afforestation, sand fixation and low-coverage desertification control has greatly improved the effect of desertification control. What particularly worth mentioning is that the waste wheat-straw and millet-straw are paved in the sand dunes like grids, in which drought-tolerant desert plants are bred or planted. This Chinese method of straw grids for sand control is known as the "miracle of the world" for its merits of drawing on local resources, low cost and obvious effect.

沙漠公路·新疆古尔班通古特沙漠
Highway in Deserts — The Gurbantunggut Desert, Xinjiang

2. 保护为本，建设自然保护区

建立自然保护区是保护我国荒漠生态系统的最重要措施。在典型的荒漠地区建立大型的自然保护区，对于保护荒漠生态系统及其野生动植物具有特殊的意义。另外，加快推进沙化土地封禁保护区的建设，严格禁止滥樵采、滥放牧、滥开垦、乱开发等破坏荒漠生态系统的活动，促进荒漠生态系统的自然修复。据大大保守的数字，我国目前已经建立的荒漠类型自然保护区 40 多个，面积超过 4000 万 km²。

2. The Establishment of Conservation-oriented Nature Reserves

The establishment of nature reserves is one of the most important measures to protect the desert ecosystems in China. The establishment of nature reserves in a typical large desert area is of special significance for the protection of desert ecosystem and wildlife. In addition, accelerating the development of desertified land enclosures reserves, strict ban on resources overexploitation, over-grazing, over-reclamation and other practices harmful to ecosystems, together with the forceful enforcement of an array of rigorous measures for curbing man-made damages, have also contributed greatly to the natural restoration of desert ecosystems. Statistics (which is a highly conservative estimation) show that over 40 desert type nature reserves have been set up across China, covering more than 40 million hectares.

希夏邦马峰下的藏野驴·西藏珠穆朗玛峰自然保护区
Equus kiang at the Foot of Shisha Pangma Mountain — Qomolangma Mountain Nature Reserve, Tibet

海市蜃楼·新疆罗布泊野骆驼自然保护区
A Mirage in the Desert — Lop Nor Nature Reserve for Wild Camels, Xinjiang

3. 沙漠公园建设

除了将荒漠生态系统典型、区位重要、保护价值突出、面临威胁严重、生态状况脆弱的荒漠区域划建为自然保护区外，还要大力发展国家沙漠公园。2013年8月，在宁夏沙坡头成立首个国家沙漠公园以来，我国已经建设沙漠公园55个。规划到2020年，要重点建设国家沙漠公园170处，总面积约67.6万hm^2，约占可治理沙化土地的2.4%。到2025年，重点建设国家沙漠公园189个，总面积约75.1万hm^2，约占可治理沙化土地的2.6%，国家沙漠公园网络体系基本建成，布局结构趋于合理，有效发挥国家沙漠公园在保护和改善荒漠生态系统中的重要作用。

3. Development of Desert Parks

In addition to the establishment of nature reserves in vulnerable areas bearing most representative, valuable, critical and seriously-endangered desert ecosystems, we should also vigorously develop national desert parks. Since the debut of Shapotou National Desert Park in Ningxia, the first among its counterparts in China, in August 2013, over 55 desert parks have been put in place across the country. It is scheduled that 170 key national desert parks will be set up by 2020, covering a total area of 676 thousand hectares, or about 2.4% of the total size of recoverable desertified lands in the country, and that 189 key national desert parks will be set up by 2025, covering a total area of 751 thousand hectares, or about 2.6% of the total size of recoverable desertified lands in the country. It is expected that a balanced, effective and comprehensive network of national desert parks will by then have been brought into existence, playing its due role and making critical contribution to the overall improvement of desert ecosystems in China.

中国第一个国家沙漠公园·宁夏沙坡头
The First National Desert Park — Shapotou, Ningxia

4. 遵循自然法则，实行综合治理

尊重荒漠生态系统内在自然规律，按照植被地带性原则和动物分布规律，荒漠生态系统遭受破坏的地方，能恢复的要尽量恢复。要"师法自然"，坚持"宜荒则荒、宜治则治、宜林则林、宜草则草"的原则。在整体科学谋划布局下，多管齐下、综合治理，采取退耕还牧、退牧还草、封滩封沙、天然植被保护等有力措施，并结合人工干预的办法，保护和提高荒漠生态系统的自我修复功能。

4. Follow the Laws of Nature and Exercise Comprehensive Control

Subject to strict observance of the natural laws of desert ecosystems, and in line with the inherent orders embodied in the distribution of fauna and flora species, all protectable areas should be put under effective protection. In addition to setting up desert type nature reserves, desert parks and other conservation-oriented sites, all places with damaged/destroyed desert ecosystems should be, to the largest possible extent, restored. We should "follow the natural laws" and adhere to the principle of reasonably treating the barren land, reasonable afforestation and planting grass according to the different circumstances. Under the overall scientific planning layout, we should adopt multi-pronged approaches and adhere to comprehensive governance. Drastic measures, such as converting farmland to pasture, converting grazing land to grassland, enclosing sandy sheet, and the integrated application of both natural recovery mechanisms and human intervention in vegetation restoring programs, should be taken in order to protect and improve the self-repairing function of the desert ecosystem.

草场改造·内蒙古锡林郭勒草原
Upgrading Grasslands — Xilingol Steppe, Inner Mongolia

5. 工程治沙，生物治理

早在 20 世纪 70 年代，我国就在"三北"地区启动三北防护林体系建设工程。进入 21 世纪以来，又先后实施了退耕还林、天然林资源保护、野生动植物保护和自然保护区建设、京津风沙源治理等重大生态修复工程，全面加快了干旱半干旱区生态治理步伐。在我国北方万里风沙线上，建起了一道乔灌草、多树种，带、片、网相结合的防护林体系，有力保护了原有的荒漠生态系统，更成了抵御风沙南侵的"绿色长城"。经过几十年的不懈努力，我国干旱半干旱区森林资源稳步增长，有效地提高了沙区植被覆盖，生态系统质量明显提升，土地沙化和水土流失等生态灾害得到有效遏制，区域生态状况和人民生产生活条件逐步改善。

5. Project-based Desertification Control and Bioremediation

As early as in the 1970s, China had already started the implementation of the Three North Shelterbelt Program in the "Three North (Northwest, North and Northeast)" region. Major ecological restoration projects including converting farmland to forest, protecting natural forest resources, protecting wildlife and developing nature reserves, controlling sand and dust storm source of Beijing and Tianjin areas have consecutively been implemented since the beginning of the 21st century, all of which have played constructive roles in restoring the arid ecosystems in the country's arid and semi-arid regions. Thanks to all these efforts, an effective shelterbelt system, composed of grasses, shrubs and trees, has emerged in the sand-ridden North China, which not only puts the desert ecosystems under its safe protection, but also provides a "Green Great Wall" that keeps south-bound wind and sand at bay. After several years of unremitting efforts, China's forest resources in arid and semi-arid areas increase steadily which effectively improves the vegetation coverage in desert areas. As a result, the overall quality of ecosystems has improved significantly, ecological disasters such as land desertification and soil erosion have been effectively curbed, and regional ecological conditions and people's production and living conditions have in turn been gradually improved.

工程治沙·内蒙古科尔沁沙地
Project-based Desertification Control—Horqin Sandy Land, Inner Mongolia

6. 社会力量参与，群策群力治沙

政府和民间携手共同防治荒漠化，社会企业团体作为公益事业积极参与和投入荒漠化防治工作，是我国荒漠化治理取得成功的重要经验之一。如"一亿棵梭梭"是阿拉善 SEE 和当地林业部门的战略合作项目，项目规划区域与政府的植被恢复区域互补，旨在使连接而成的绿化带成为一道生态屏障，遏制腾格里、乌兰布和、巴丹吉林三大沙漠接合和进一步蔓延，确保有效恢复当地荒漠植被。在阿拉善 SEE 苏海图嘎查项目示范区，自 2014 年至今已恢复梭梭 11.2 万亩，有效地改善了当地生态环境。

6. Participatory Approaches for Combating Desertification

A key ingredient for China's success in combating desertification lies in its emphasis on close cooperation between the governments and the non-governmental sectors, in which the role of various social organizations, businesses and public welfare entities are brought to their respective fullest play. The "*Haloxylon* 100,000,000" project, a strategic cooperative initiative between SEE Foundation and local forestry department to establish a green shelterbelt that prevents the Badan Jaran Desert, the Tengger Desert, and the Ulan Buh Desert from joining and further spreading, is just a case in point that testifies to the mutually complimentary effect of public-private cooperation in desert vegetation recovery. Approximately 112,000 *mu* of *Haloxylon* have been restored under the SEE Foundation Suhaitu Demonstrative Project since the inception of this initiative in 2014, which has played a highly constructive role in improving local eco-environment.

阿拉善 SEE 一亿棵梭梭项目·苏海图示范区
SEE Foundation "*Haloxylon* 100,000,000" Project — Suhaitu Demontrative Project Area

沙产业——肉苁蓉培植·内蒙古阿拉善左旗
Desert-based Industry, Cultivation of Cistanche deserticola — Alxa Left Banner, Inner Mongolia

一带一路建设·新疆阿拉山口
The Belt and Road Initiative — the Alataw Pass, Xinjiang

7. 发展沙产业，沙区精准扶贫

我国沙区与集中连片的特困地区契合度高，沙区贫困人口占全国贫困人口总数的30%。沙区生存环境恶劣，自然承载力低下，人们在这里不仅要和风沙抗争，更要与贫困抗争。坚持保护优先、合理利用的原则，因地制宜发展沙产业，是沙区各地探索出的治沙新动力。以治沙带扶贫、带致富，以开发促保护，是近年来沙区人民探索出的一条有效路径。如图为梭梭根部嫁接肉苁蓉，将生态价值与经济价值有机结合，在解决荒漠化问题的同时为当地老百姓增收。

7. Developing Deserticulture and Carrying out Targeted Poverty-alleviating Projects in Sandy Areas

There is a high correlation between China's sandy areas and its poverty-stricken areas, and the poor population living in the desert-prevalent areas accounts for 30% of the total poor population throughout the China. Sandy areas are typically endowed with undesirable living environment and low natural carrying capacity. People there not only have to fight against wind and sand, but also struggle against poverty. Adhering to the principle of giving priority to protection and reasonable utilization, development of deserticulture according to local conditions is a new impetus for desert control in sandy areas. Supporting the poor and acquiring wealth along with controlling sand; promoting protection along with exploitation is an effective way explored by the people in sandy areas over the past years. Through the application of an innovative technique that implants *Cistanche deserticola* to *Haloxylon* roots and hence taps into their respective values for ecology and economy at the same time, a sound solution has been found to tackle desertification and improve livelihood of local people simultaneously.

8. 国际合作，一带一路

中国作为《联合国防治荒漠化公约》缔约国，积极履行公约规定的义务，"一带一路"所涉及的60多个国家都是《联合国防治荒漠化公约》缔约方，都不同程度地遭受着荒漠化、土地退化和干旱的危害，是世界上荒漠化问题最严重的地区之一，因此，推进荒漠化防治共同行动，大力推进"一带一路"的防沙治沙，扩大国际合作，共享防治经验，为沿线国家提供"中国模式"尤为重要。

8. International Cooperation and the Belt and Road Initiative

As a party to the *United Nations Convention to Combat Desertification* (UNCCD), China has been earnestly and consistently fulfilling its obligations. The 60 plus countries involved in "the Belt and Road Initiative" are all contracting parties to the *United Nations Convention to Combat Desertification* (UNCCD), and at the same time are all suffering to a more or less degree from serious problems inflicted by desertification, land degradation and drought. For this reason, it is particularly important to promote international cooperation in the prevention and control of desertification under "the Belt and Road Initiative", so that the "Chinese Model" for addressing this global challenge can be shared by more countries along the way.

物种简介
Introduction of Species

为了便于读者进一步了解物种情况和查阅，此部分列出了在本书中出现的物种及其中文名、拉丁学名、保护级别、濒危程度等，还标上了该物种在书中出现的页码。

简写情况如下：

CHINA I = 国家一级保护野生动（植）物
CHINA II = 国家二级保护野生动（植）物
IUCN EW = IUCN物种红色名录等级，野外灭绝
IUCN CR = IUCN物种红色名录等级，极危
IUCN EN = IUCN物种红色名录等级，濒危
IUCN VU = IUCN物种红色名录等级，易危
IUCN NT = IUCN物种红色名录等级，近危
IUCN LC = IUCN物种红色名录等级，无危
CITES I = CITES附录 I 物种
CITES II = CITES附录 II 物种
CITES III = CITES附录 III 物种

注：
● 为保护野生动植物，维护生态平衡，我国先后颁布了《中华人民共和国野生动物保护法》和《中华人民共和国野生植物保护条例》，其中规定国家对珍贵、濒危的野生动植物实行重点保护，并根据物种的珍贵濒危程度和管理严格要求依次分为一级保护和二级保护（简写为CHINA I 和CHINA II）。
● 世界自然保护联盟（简称IUCN）是目前世界上最大的、最重要的世界性保护联盟。IUCN编制的《濒危物种红色名录》是被广泛接受和使用的受威胁物种分级标准体系。该组织每年评估数以千计物种的绝种风险，将物种编入9个不同的保护级别：依次为灭绝（EX）、野外灭绝（EW）、极危（CR）、濒危（EN）、易危（VU）、近危（NT）、无危（LC）、数据缺乏（DD）和未予评估（NE）。
● 《濒危野生动植物物种国际贸易公约》（以下简称《公约》）是全球缔约国之间为了保护野生动植物物种不至于由于国际贸易而遭到过度开发利用而进行的国际合作。《公约》将受管理的野生动植物物种按照其物种状况及其受贸易影响的严重程度依次列为附录I、附录II和附录III名单（简写为CITES I、CITES II和CITES III）。
● IUCN采用IUCN官网（http://www.iucnredlist.org/search）确定，评定等级均为Ver. 3.1版本。
● CITES采用2017年4月4日修订的版本（https://cites.org/sites/default/files/eng/app/2017/E-Appendices-2017-04-04.pdf）。

This part has listed all the species introduced in this book for reference. The introduction indicates their Chinese names, Latin names, grades of protection and degrees of endangered condition. It also shows the number of pages where the specific species are introduced.

The abbreviations are as follows:

CHINA I = Wild Fauna and Flora under the 1st Grade National Protection
CHINA II = Wild Fauna and Flora under the 2nd Grade National Protection
IUCN EW = Extinct Species in the Wild of the IUCN Red List of Threatened Species
IUCN CR = Critically Endangered Species of the IUCN Red List of Threatened Species
IUCN EN = Endangered Species of the IUCN Red List of Threatened Species
IUCN VU = Vulnerable Species of the IUCN Red List of Threatened Species
IUCN NT = Near Threatened Species of the IUCN Red List of Threatened Species
IUCN LC = Least Concern Species of the IUCN Red List of Threatened Species
CITES I = Species listed in Appendices I of Convention on International Trade in Endangered Species of Wild Fauna and Flora (CITES)
CITES II = Species listed in Appendices II of Convention on International Trade in Endangered Species of Wild Fauna and Flora (CITES)
CITES III = Species listed in Appendices III of Convention on International Trade in Endangered Species of Wild Fauna and Flora (CITES)

Note:

In order to protect wild animals and plants and maintain the ecological balance, the Chinese government has successively promulgated the Law of the People's Republic of China on the Protection of Wild Animals and the Regulations of the People's Republic of China on the Protection of Wild Plants, which stipulate that the Chinese government protects the rare and endangered wild animals and plants, and categorized the species as CHINA I and CHINA II according to its degree of rareness and endangered condition, as well as the management requirement.

The World Conservation Union (IUCN) is currently the largest and most important world union for the protection of wild fauna and flora. The IUCN *Red List of Threatened Species* is a widely accepted and applied system. The IUCN carries out an annual evaluation on extinction risk of more than 1000 species and categorizes the species into nine different protection levels according to the evaluation: Extinct (EX), Extinct in the Wild (EW), Critically Endangered (CR), Endangered (EN), Vulnerable (VU), Near Threatened (NT), Least Concern (LC), Data Deficient (DD), and Not Evaluated (NE). (The ranking system adopts Ver. 3.1 in this album. http://www.iucnredlist.org/search.)

The Convention on International Trade in Endangered Species of Wild Fauna and Flora (CITES) is an international agreement between contracting parties aiming at ensuring that international trade in species of wild animals and plants does not threaten their survival. The species covered by CITES are listed in the appendices I, II and III (abbreviated as CITES I, CITES II and CITES III) according to the situation of the species and the degree of influence from trading. (https://cites.org/sites/default/files/eng/app/2017/E-Appendices-2017-04-04.pdf.)

岩羊
Pseudois nayaur
CHINA II, IUCN LC
Page: 8, 134, 196

野骆驼
Camelus ferus
CHINA I, IUCN CR
Page: 12

蓑羽鹤
Anthropoides virgo
CHINA II, IUCN LC
Page: 39

榆树
Ulmus pumila
Page: 40, 49

黄柳
Salix gordejevii
Page: 47

沙米
Agriophyllum squarrosum
Page: 47

沙芥
Pugionium cornutum
Page: 49

丹顶鹤
Grus japonensis
CHINA I, IUCN EN, CITES I
Page: 50

白枕鹤
Grus vipio
CHINA II, IUCN VU, CITES I
Page: 51

黄鼠
Spermophilus sp.
IUCN LC
Page: 52

蜣螂
Catharsius sp.
Page: 52

沙蜥
Phrynocephalus sp.
Page: 52

草原雕
Aquila nipalensis
CHINA II, IUCN EN
Page: 52

大鸨
Otis tarda
CHINA I, IUCN VU
Page: 53

沙地樟子松
Pinus sylvestris var. *mongolica*
Page: 59

毛腿沙鸡
Syrrhaptes paradoxus
IUCN LC
Page: 59

梭梭
Haloxylon ammodendron
Page: 66, 106, 141

肉苁蓉
Cistanche deserticola
Page: 66, 211

白刺
Nitraria tangutorum
Page: 66, 106

花棒
Hedysarum scoparium
Page: 66

沙地云杉
Picea mongolica
Page: 67

狼
Canis lupus
IUCN LC, CITES II
Page: 68

赤狐
Vulpes vulpes
IUCN LC
Page: 69

雪鸮
Bubo scandiacus
CHINA II, IUCN LC
Page: 70

石鸡
Alectoris chukar
IUCN LC
Page: 71, 156

遗鸥
Larus relictus
CHINA I, IUCN VU, CITES I
Page: 72

黄爪隼
Falco naumanni
CHINA II, IUCN LC
Page: 73

黑琴鸡
Lyrurus tetrix
CHINA II, IUCN LC
Page: 74

长尾林鸮
Strix uralensis
CHINA II, IUCN LC
Page: 75

骆驼刺
Alhagi sparsifolia
Page: 85, 154, 179

大天鹅
Cygnus cygnus
CHINA II, IUCN LC
Page: 90, 168, 204

胡杨
Populus euphratica
Page: 102, 103, 128

沙枣
Elaeagnus angustifolia
Page: 106

盐爪爪
Kalidium foliatum
Page: 106

海韭菜
Triglochin maritimum
Page: 106

红砂
Reaumuria songarica
Page: 106

羽毛三芒草
Aristida pennata
Page: 107

高鼻羚羊
Saiga tatarica
CHINA I, IUCN CR, CITES II
Page: 108

膜果麻黄
Ephedra przewalskii
Page: 119

八哥
Acridotheres cristatellus
Page: 119

盘羊
Ovis ammon
CHINA II, IUCN NT
Page: 130, 132, 157

棕尾鵟
Buteo rufinus
CHINA II, IUCN LC
Page: 133

普氏野马
Equus ssp. *przewalskii*
CHINA I, IUCN EN
Page: 134, 136

蒙古野驴
Equus hemionus
CHINA I, IUCN NT, CITES II
Page: 134

天山马鹿
Cervus elaphus songaricus
China II
Page: 134

鹅喉羚
Gazella subgutturosa
CHINA II, IUCN VU
Page: 135, 182

红柳
Salix wilsonii
Page: 145

盐角草
Salicornia europaea
Page: 154

沙蓬
Agriophyllum squarrosum
Page: 154

猪毛菜
Salsola collina
Page: 154

猫头刺
Oxytropis aciphylla
Page: 155

沙棘
Hippophae rhamnoides
Page: 165

藏羚羊
Pantholops hodgsonii
CHINA I, IUCN NT, CITES I
Page: 165, 184

垫状植物
Cushion Plants
Page: 178

地衣
Lichens
Page: 178

大黄
Rheum sp.
Page: 178

苞叶雪莲
Saussurea obvallata
Page: 178

高山兀鹫
Gyps himalayensis
CHINA II, IUCN NT
Page: 180

小嘴乌鸦
Corvus corone
IUCN LC
Page: 180

金雕
Aquila chrysaetos
CHINA I, IUCN LC
Page: 181

碱蓬
Suaeda glauca
Page: 182

鼠兔
Ochotona sp.
Page: 183

胡兀鹫
Gypaetus barbatus
CHINA II, IUCN NT
Page: 183

蟾蜍
Bufo sp.
Page: 183

雪鸡
Tetraogallus sp.
CHINA II
Page: 183

北山羊
Capra sibirica
CHINA I, IUCN LC
Page: 185

雪豹
Panthera uncia
CHINA I, IUCN EN, CITES I
Page: 186

褐背拟地鸦
Pseudopodoces humilis
IUCN LC
Page: 187

藏野驴
Equus kiang
CHINA I, IUCN LC, CITES II
Page: 188

普氏原羚
Procapra przewlskii
CHINA I, IUCN CR
Page: 190, 191

喜马拉雅旱獭
Marmota himalayana
IUCN LC
Page: 192

野牦牛
Bos mutus
CHINA I, IUCN VU, CITES I
Page: 193